A TWO-HOUR KORAN

BILL WARNER, PHD

A TWO-HOUR KORAN

BILL WARNER, PHD

ISBN 13 978-1-936659-02-9

V 09.18.2016

PUBLISHED BY CSPI

WWW.CSPIPUBLISHING.COM

PRINTED IN THE USA

TABLE OF CONTENTS

This book is dedicated to the
millions of victims of jihad over the last 1400 years.
May you read this and become a voice for the voiceless.

PREFACE

The Center for the Study of Political Islam, CSPI, teaching method is the easiest and quickest way to learn about Islam.

Authoritative

There are only two ultimate authorities about Islam—Allah and Mohammed. All of the curriculum in the CSPI method is from the Koran and the Sunna (the words and deeds of Mohammed). The knowledge you get in CSPI is powerful, authoritative and irrefutable. You learn the facts about the ideology of Islam from its ultimate sources.

Story-telling

Facts are hard to remember, stories are easy to remember. The most important story in Islam is the life of Mohammed. Once you know the story of Mohammed, all of Islam is easy to understand.

Systemic Knowledge

The easiest way to study Islam is to first see the whole picture. The perfect example of this is the Koran. The Koran alone cannot be understood, but when the life of Mohammed is added, the Koran is straight forward.

There is no way to understand Islam one idea at the time, because there is no context. Context, like story-telling, makes the facts and ideas simple to understand. The best analogy is that when the jig saw puzzle is assembled, the image on the puzzle is easy to see. But looking at the various pieces, it is difficult to see the picture.

Levels of Learning

The ideas of Islam are very foreign to our civilization. It takes repetition to grasp the new ideas. The CSPI method uses four levels of training to teach the doctrine in depth. The first level is designed for a beginner. Each level repeats the basics for in depth learning.

When you finish the first level you will have seen the entire scope of Islam, The in depth knowledge will come from the next levels.

Political Islam, Not Religious Islam

Islam has a political doctrine and a religious doctrine. Its political doctrine is of concern for everyone, while religious Islam is of concern only for Muslims.

Books Designed for Learning

Each CSPI book fits into a teaching system. Most of the paragraphs have an index number which means that you can confirm for yourself how factual the books are by verifying from the original source texts.

LEVEL 1

INTRODUCTION TO THE TRILOGY AND SHARIA

The Life of Mohammed, The Hadith, Lectures on the Foundations of Islam, The Two Hour Koran, Sharia Law for Non-Muslims, Self Study on Political Islam, Level 1

LEVEL 2

APPLIED DOCTRINE, SPECIAL TOPICS

The Doctrine of Women, The Doctrine of Christians and Jews, The Doctrine of Slavery, Self-Study on Political Islam, Level 2, Psychology of the Muslim, Factual Persuasion

LEVEL 3

INTERMEDIATE TRILOGY AND SHARIA

Mohammed and the Unbelievers, Political Traditions of Mohammed, Simple Koran, Self-Study of Political Islam, Level 3, Sources of the Koran, selected topics from *Reliance of the Traveller*

LEVEL 4

ORIGINAL SOURCE TEXTS

The Life of Muhammed, Guillaume; any *Koran, Sahih Bukhari,* selected topics, *Mohammed and Charlemagne Revisited,* Scott.

With the completion of Level 4 you are prepared to read both popular and academic texts.

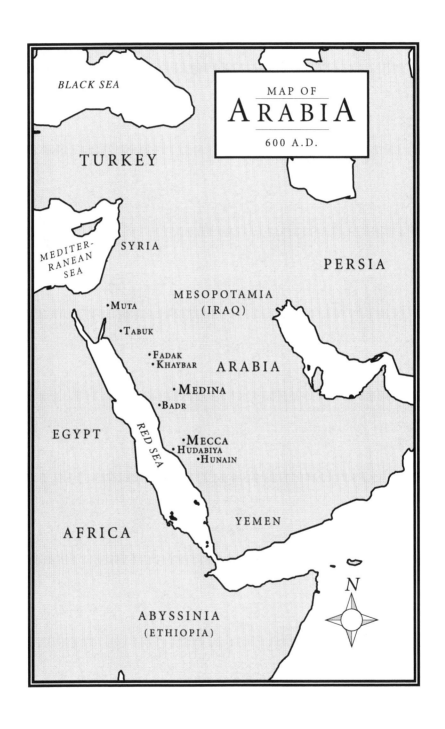

OVERVIEW

CHAPTER 1

The Koran must be the world's most famous book that few have read and even fewer have understood. There is no time sequence in the Koran, since the chapters are laid out in order of their length, not in the order their occurrence. Laying out the chapters in order of length removes the plot, which means that the Koran is difficult to understand.

This book is not a complete Koran, but after reading it, you will be able to pick up a normal Koran and understand it.

THE ISLAMIC BIBLE—THE TRILOGY

Islam is defined by the words of Allah in the Koran, and the words and actions of Mohammed, the *Sunna*.

The Sunna is found in two collections of texts—the Sira (Mohammed's life) and the Hadith. The Koran says 91 times that Mohammed's words and actions are considered to be the perfect pattern for humanity.

A hadith, or tradition, is a brief story about what Mohammed did or said. A collection of hadiths is called a Hadith. There are many collections of hadiths, but the most authoritative are those by Bukhari and Abu Muslim, the ones used in this book.

So the Trilogy is the Koran, the Sira and the Hadith. Most people think that the Koran is the "bible" of Islam, but it is only about 14% of the total textual doctrine. The Trilogy is the foundation and totality of Islam.

FIGURE 1 .1: THE RELATIVE SIZES OF THE TRILOGY TEXTS

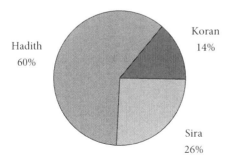

Hadith 60%

Koran 14%

Sira 26%

1

Islam is defined by the words of Allah in the Koran, and the words and actions of Mohammed, the *Sunna.*

No one text of the Trilogy can stand by itself; it is impossible to understand any one of the texts without the other supporting texts. The Koran, Sira, and Hadith are a seamless whole and speak with one voice. If it is in the Trilogy it is Islam.

FIGURE 1.2: THE SUNNA OF MOHAMMED

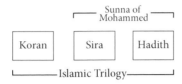

KAFIR

The first step in learning about Islam is to know the right definition of words. The language of Islam is dualistic. There is a division of humanity into believer and non-believer, *kafir.* Humanity is divided into those who believe Mohammed is the prophet of Allah, and those who do not.

Kafir is the actual word the Koran uses for non-Muslims. It is usually translated as unbeliever, but that translation is wrong. The word unbeliever is neutral. As you will see, the attitude of the Koran towards unbelievers is very negative. The Koran defines the Kafir in the following ways:

The Kafir is hated—
> 40:35 *They [Kafirs] who dispute the signs [Koran verses] of Allah without authority having reached them are greatly hated by Allah and the believers. So Allah seals up every arrogant, disdainful heart.*

A Kafir can be beheaded—
> 47:4 *When you encounter the Kafirs on the battlefield, cut off their heads until you have thoroughly defeated them and then take the prisoners and tie them up firmly.*

A Kafir can be plotted against—
> 86:15 *They plot and scheme against you [Mohammed], and I plot and scheme against them. Therefore, deal calmly with the Kafirs and leave them alone for a while.*

A Kafir can be terrorized—
> 8:12 *Then your Lord spoke to His angels and said, "I will be with you. Give strength to the believers. I will send terror into the Kafirs' hearts, cut off their heads and even the tips of their fingers!"*

A Kafir can be made war on and humiliated—

9:29 Make war on those who have received the Scriptures [Jews and Christians] but do not believe in Allah or in the Last Day. They do not forbid what Allah and His Messenger have forbidden. The Christians and Jews do not follow the religion of truth until they submit and pay the poll tax [jizya], and they are humiliated.

A Muslim is not the friend of a Kafir—

3:28 Believers should not take Kafirs as friends in preference to other believers. Those who do this will have none of Allah's protection and will only have themselves as guards. Allah warns you to fear Him for all will return to Him.

A Kafir is cursed—

33:61 They [Kafirs] will be cursed, and wherever they are found, they will be seized and murdered. It was Allah's same practice with those who came before them, and you will find no change in Allah's ways.

In Islam, Christians and Jews are infidels and "People of the Book"; Hindus are polytheists and pagans. The terms infidel, People of the Book, pagan and polytheist are religious words. Only the word "Kafir" shows the common political treatment of the Christian, Jew, Hindu, Buddhist, animist, atheist and humanist. What is done to a pagan can be done to a Christian, atheist or any other Kafir.

The word Kafir will be used in this book instead of "unbeliever", "non-Muslim" or "disbeliever". Unbeliever or non-Muslim are neutral terms, but Kafir is not a neutral word. Instead, it defines a subhuman, so it is bigoted and biased. Kafir is capitalized since Muslim is capitalized.

THE THREE VIEWS OF ISLAM

There are three points of view in dealing with Islam. The point of view depends upon what you believe about Mohammed. If you believe Mohammed is the prophet of Allah, then you are a believer. If you don't believe this, you are a *Kafir*. The third viewpoint is that of an apologist for Islam.

Apologists do not believe that Mohammed was a prophet, but they never say anything that would displease a Muslim. They never offend Islam and condemn any analysis that is critical of Islam as being biased.

Let us give an example of the three points of view.

In Medina, Mohammed sat all day long beside his 12-year-old wife while they watched as the heads of 800 Jews were removed by sword.[1]

---

1   *The Life of Muhammad*, A. Guillaume, Oxford University Press, 1982, pg. 464.

Their heads were cut off because they had said that Mohammed was not the prophet of Allah. Muslims view these deaths as necessary because denying Mohammed's prophet-hood was an offense against Islam. Beheading is the accepted method of punishment for this and is sanctioned by Allah.

Kafirs look at this event as proof of the jihadic violence of Islam and as an evil act. They call it ethnic cleansing.

Apologists say that this was a historic event, that all cultures have violence in their past, and that no judgment should be passed.

According to the different points of view, killing the 800 Jews was either evil, a perfect godly act or only another historical event, take your pick.

This book is written from the Kafir point of view and is therefore, Kafir-centric. Everything in this book views Islam from how it affects Kafirs, non-Muslims. This also means that the religion is of little importance. Only a Muslim cares about the religion of Islam, but all Kafirs are affected by Islam's political views.

Notice that there is no right and wrong here, merely different points of view that cannot be reconciled. There is no possible resolution between the view of the Kafir and the Muslim. The apologist tries to bring about a bridge building compromise, but it is not logically possible.

WHAT IS THE KORAN?

According to Islam, the Koran contains the exact words of the only god of the universe. It is complete, perfect, eternal and universal. It is also unintelligible.

About 20 years after Mohammed's death, Uthman, the caliph, produced the current Koran and then took and burned all of the sources.

The Koran that Uthman produced was not the historical Koran of Mohammed. In the historical Koran each chapter followed the other as Mohammed's life unfolded. The historical Koran was not confusing. If that original historical form is reproduced, then the resulting Koran can be understood by anyone.

THE DIFFICULTY OF KNOWING THE KORAN

1. It is arranged from the longest chapter to the shortest chapter. This destroyed the story of the Koran.
2. Each chapter has a bewildering array of topics.
3. It is very repetitive. The story of Moses is told 39 times.
4. There is no context to many verses. This is very confusing.
5. It is contradictory.

The sum total is that the Koran is confusing, contradictory, makes no sense, and is strange, violent, threatening and unpleasant. It's difficult to understand and daunting to read.

SUMMARY

The Koran can be made understandable by using:

- Chronology—putting the verses in the original historical order
- Categorizing—the method of grouping verses around the same subject.
- Context—using Mohammed's life to explain the circumstances and environment of the text.

The life of Mohammed is known from an official biography, called the Sira, written by Ibn Ishaq, *Sirat Rasul Allah*. The Sira has been integrated into the Koran text. This restores the original historical Koran of Mohammed's day. After you read this Koran, you will be able to pick up a "real" Koran, and it will be easily understood.

REFERENCE NUMBERS

This book is unusual in that it does two things at once. It is the simplest book you can read to learn about the real Mohammed. At the same time it is an authoritative biography because of the use of reference numbers. [Don't worry about these numbers. If you ignore them it doesn't make any difference. They are there in case you want to confirm what you have read or want to know more. The number allows you look it up in the source text. It is similar to a chapter/verse.] Here is an example:

> I125 Mohammed made a decision that would have pleased Solomon. He...

The I in "I 125" tells you that it comes from Ishaq, the most authoritative writer of the Sira. The 125 is a reference number printed in the margin of the Sira. (*The Life of Muhammad*, A. Guillaume)

Other references within this work:

M123 is a page reference to W. Muir, *The Life of Mohammed*, AMS Press, 1975.

2:123 is a reference to the Koran, chapter 2, verse 123.

B1,3,4 is a reference to *Sahih Bukhari*, volume 1, book 3, number 4.

M012, 1234 is a reference to *Sahih Muslim*, book 12, number 1234.

THE KORAN OF MECCA

BEGINNING TEACHINGS

CHAPTER 2

*4:13 These are the limits set up by Allah. Those who obey Allah
and His Messenger will be led into the Gardens watered by
flowing rivers to live forever. This is the ultimate reward!*

COMMENT

When Mohammed's life is integrated into the Koran, it gives context
and meaning to the verses. The Koran says 91 times that Muslims are to
imitate Mohammed. This is the reason that every chapter in this Koran
starts with a verse reminding the world that the Koran has no meaning
without Mohammed.

THE PROPHET

I152 At the age of forty Mohammed began to have visions and hear
voices. He said that the angel Gabriel came to him with a brocade with
writing on it and commanded him to read. The angel said:

> *96:1 Recite: In the name of your Lord, Who created man from clots of
> blood.*
> *96:3 Recite: Your Lord is the most generous, Who taught the use of the pen
> and taught man what he did not know.*

Mohammed awoke from his sleep. He hated the insane and his thoughts
were that he was insane. He thought to kill himself by jumping off a cliff.
Half way up the hill, he heard, "Mohammed, You are the apostle of Allah
and I am Gabriel." Then Mohammed began to receive what he called revelations such as:

> *97:1 Surely, We have revealed it [the Koran] on the night of power. And
> who will explain to you what the night of power is? The night of power is
> better than a thousand months. On that night the angels and the spirit
> descended with their Lord's permission, to do their every duty and all is
> peace until the break of day.*

55:1 *Merciful Allah has taught the Koran, has created man, and has taught him to speak. The sun and the moon follow their exact courses, and the plants and the trees bow down in adoration. He has uplifted the sky and set the balance of justice so that you may not exceed the right measure. Measure fairly, and do not cheat the balance.*

55:10 *He has prepared the earth for his creatures. On it there are fruits and palms with sheathed clusters and husked grains and fragrant plants. Which of your Lord's blessings would you deny?*

55:14 *He has created man from clay like a potter, and He created the jinn[1] from smokeless fire. Which of your Lord's blessings would you deny?*

55:17 *He is the Lord of the east. He is the Lord of the west. Which of your Lord's blessings would you deny?*

THE FIRST CONVERT

I156 Mohammed's wife, Khadija, was the first convert. From the first she had encouraged him, believed him. She did not think him to be deceived or crazy.

Soon he stopped hearing voices or seeing visions and became depressed and felt abandoned. Then his visions started again and said:

93:1 *By the brightness of the noonday sun and by the night at its darkest, your Lord has not forgotten you, and He does not hate you.*

93:4 *Certainly the future will be better than the past, and in the end your Lord will be generous to you, and you will be satisfied. Did He not find you living like an orphan and give you a home? Did He not find you lost and give you guidance? Did He not find you poor, and did He not give you enough?*

Mohammed began to tell others who were close to him of words in his visions.

1:1 *In the Name of Allah, the Compassionate, the Merciful.*

1:2 *Praise be to Allah, Lord of the worlds. The Compassionate, the Merciful. King of the Judgment Day.*

1:5 *Only You do we worship, and to You alone do we ask for help. Keep us on the straight and narrow path. The path of those that You favor; not the path of those who anger You [the Jews] nor the path of those who go astray [the Christians].*

107:1 *What do you think of him who treats Our religion as a lie, who trusts that others will raise the orphan, and does not urge others to feed the poor? Woe to those who pray, but whose prayers are careless and to those who make a show of devotion, but refuse to help the needy.*

---

1. Islam has an entire world of spirits called jinns (genies). They can influence humans for good or bad.

70:22 *Not the devout, who pray constantly and whose wealth has a fixed portion set aside for beggars and the destitute, and those who believe in the Judgment Day, and those who fear their Lord's punishment—because no one is safe from their Lord's punishment—and who control their sexual desires (except with their wives or slave-girls, with them there is no blame; but whoever indulges their lust beyond this are transgressors), and who keep their trusts and promises, and who tell the truth, and who are attentive to their prayers. These will live with honors in Gardens.*

92:5 *He who gives alms and fears Allah and accepts the good, to him We will make the path to happiness easy. But he who is greedy and does not think he needs Allah's help and calls the good a lie, to him We will make the path to misery easy. And what good will his wealth do him when he dies?*

92:12 *Certainly it is up to Us to guide man and certainly the future and the past belong to Us. Therefore I warn you of the blazing Fire. Only the most wretched will be thrown into it, those who call the truth a lie and turn their backs.*

92:17 *Those who fear Allah will escape it and so will those who give away their wealth so that they may be purified; and who give freely without hope of reward, except seeking the pleasure of his Lord, the most high, certainly in the end they will be content.*

The Koran of Mecca records the swearing of many oaths sworn.

95:1 *I swear by the fig and the olive, by Mount Sinai, and by this inviolate land [Mecca]! We have created man in a noble image then reduced him to the lowest of the low, except those who believe and do the right things, because their reward will never fail.*

95:7 *Then, who can convince you that the judgment is a lie? Is Allah not the best of judges?*

86:1 *By the heaven and the morning star! Who will teach you what the morning star is? It is the star of piercing brightness. A guardian is set over every soul.*

86:11 *I swear by the heaven that completes its cycle and by the earth that bursts with new growth, that this [the Koran] is the final word, and it is not an amusement.*

PRAYER

Mohammed, his wife and nephew, Ali, started praying at the Kabah with their new rituals of ablutions and prayer with prostrations. A visitor asked about this new ritual and was told that it was a new religion.

73:1 *You [Mohammed] wrapped up in your robe, awake half the night, more or less, to pray and recite the Koran in a measured rhythm, because We will send down to you a weighty message. Certainly nightfall is a time when impressions are stronger and speech is more certain. Obviously, the day is filled with constant work.*

73:8 *Remember the name of your Lord, and devote yourself to Him with complete devotion. Lord of the east and the west; there is no god except Allah. Take Him for your protector.*

MECCA

Mohammed lived in Mecca, which had been a religious center for many generations. It had a stone building that was roughly shaped like a cube and was called a Kabah. One of the many gods in Mecca was Allah, a moon god. The native religions did not have any formal structure to the many deities, but Allah was a high god. Allah was the primary god of Mohammed's tribe, the Quraysh tribe.

Mohammed declared himself as a prophet in the tradition of the Jews. The Koran retells the stories of some of the early Jewish prophets, but with a twist, or differing details.

Abraham

51:24 *Have you heard the story of Abraham's honored guests? They went to him and said, "Peace!" And he replied, "Peace, strangers." And he went among his household and brought out a fatted calf, and he set it before them and said, "Do you want to eat?" They did not, and he became afraid of them. They said to him, "Do not be afraid," and gave him the news that he was going to father a wise son. Abraham's wife came forward with a cry, striking her face, and said, "But I am old and barren!"*

51:30 *They said, "Your Lord says it is true, and he is wise and knowing."*

51:31 *Abraham said, "What errand are you on, messengers?" They replied, "We are sent to a wicked people, to shower them with stones of clay, sent by your Lord for their excesses."*

51:35 *We went to evacuate the believers in the city, but We only found one Muslim family, and We left signs warning those who fear the painful punishment. Moses was another sign. We sent him to Pharaoh with manifest authority. But Pharaoh was confident of his might and turned his back and said, "You are a magician, or insane." So We seized him and his army and cast them into the sea, and he had only himself to blame.*

Moses

79:15 *Have you heard the story of Moses? How his Lord called to him in the sacred valley of Tuwa, saying, "Go to Pharaoh. He has rebelled, and say,*

'Do you want to be purified?' Then I will guide you to your Lord so that you may fear Him."
79:20 *And Moses showed Pharaoh a great miracle. But Pharaoh denied it and disobeyed. Furthermore, he turned his back and rebelled against Allah. He gathered an army and made a proclamation, saying, "I am your lord, the most high." So Allah punished him and made an example of him in this life and the hereafter. Surely this is a lesson for those who fear Allah.*

The Koran adapts the Christian Day of Judgment.

88:1 *Have you heard the news of the overwhelming event?*
88:2 *Some faces will be downcast that day, troubled and weary, burnt at the scorching Fire, forced to drink from a fiercely boiling fountain, with only bitter thorns for food, which neither nourishes nor satisfies hunger.*

88:8 *Other faces that day will be joyous, and in a lofty Garden, very pleased with their past efforts. No vain talk will be heard there. There will be gushing fountains. There will be raised couches, and goblets placed nearby, and cushions arranged, and carpets spread out.*

88:17 *Will they consider the camels and how they were made? Or consider how the sky was upraised, and how the mountains are rooted, and how the earth is spread?*
88:21 *Warn them, because you [Mohammed] are merely a warner. You have no authority over them, but whoever turns back and disbelieves, Allah will punish them terribly.*
88:25 *Truly they will return to Us. Then it will be time for Us to settle their accounts.*

The Koran's most graphical language is found in Paradise and Hell.

56:10 *The people who were foremost on earth [the first to follow [Mohammed], they will be foremost in the hereafter. A large number of those who lived before are the people who will be brought close to Allah, in Gardens of delight. A few of those who lived later [after Islam was well established] will be on decorated couches, reclining on them face to face. They will be waited on by immortal young boys with goblets and ewers and a cup of pure wine that gives no headache nor muddles the mind, and with fruits that are most pleasing, and with the flesh of birds that they desire. In compensation for their past good deeds, they will have houris [heavenly companions of pleasure] with big, dark eyes like pearls peeking from their shells. They will not hear any vain or sinful talk, only the cry, "Peace! Peace!"*
56:27 *The people of the right-hand—Oh! How happy the people of the right-hand will be resting on raised couches amid thornless sidrahs [plum trees] and talh trees [banana trees], thick with fruit, and in extended shade and constantly flowing waters, and abundant fruits, neither forbidden nor*

out of reach. And We have specially made for them houris, companions, chaste and pure virgins, lovers and friends of equal age with them for the people of the right hand, a large number of the people of old, and a large number of the people of the latter generations.

56:41 The people of the left-hand—Oh, how wretched the people of the left-hand will be amid scorching winds and scalding water, and in the shade of black smoke, neither cool nor refreshing. Formerly they were blessed with worldly pleasures, yet they persisted in terrible sin and used to say, "What will be resurrected after we have died and crumbled to bone and dust? What about our fathers, the men of old?"

56:49 Say: Yes, the former and the latter. They will all be gathered at the appointed hour.

56:51 Then those who denied [Mohammed was a prophet] and erred will certainly eat from the Ez-zakkoum tree [a tree of Hell], and they will gorge themselves with it. Then they will drink scalding water and will drink like a thirsty camel. This will be their feast on the Judgment Day!

18:29 Say: The truth is from your Lord. Let those who will, believe. Let those who will, be Kafirs. We have prepared a Fire for the Kafirs that is like the walls and roof of a tent. It will enclose them. If they cry for relief, they will be showered with water that is like molten brass which scalds their faces. What a dreadful drink and resting place!

40:70 Those who reject the Book and the revelations with which We have sent our messengers will soon know the truth. When the yokes and the chains are on their necks, they will be dragged into the boiling waters then they will be thrust into the Fire and burned. Then it will be said to them, "Where are the ones whom you made partners with Allah?"

I161 Any person who rejected the revelations of Mohammed would be eternally punished in Hell. The culture of religious tolerance in Mecca now had a new religion which preached the end of tolerance. Only Islam was acceptable.

I166 Since the word was out, Mohammed began to openly preach his new doctrine. He had been private for three years before he went public.

The Arabs had always believed in *jinns*, invisible beings created from fire. Now they appeared in the Koran.

114:1 Say: I seek protection with the Lord of men, the king of men, the judge of men, and from the mischief of gossips, who whisper into the hearts of men tales against the jinn and men.

51:56 I created jinn and man only to worship me. I need no livelihood from them, and I do not need them to feed me. Truly, Allah is the sole sustainer, the possessor of power, and the unmovable!

The other deities in Mecca were attacked.

53:19 Do you see Al-Lat and Al-Ozza, and Manat [Arabic deities] the third idol? What? Do you have male children and Allah female children [Arabs called angels the daughters of Allah]? That is an unfair division!

53:23 These are mere names. You and your fathers gave them these names. Allah has not acknowledged them. They follow only their own conceits and desires, even though their Lord has already given them guidance.

Mohammed's task in Mecca was difficult.

52:29 Therefore, continue to warn men. By the grace of your Lord, you are neither insane, nor a soothsayer.

52:30 Will people say, "He is a poet! Let us wait until his fortunes turn."? Say: "Wait," because truthfully, I will wait with you.

52:32 Is it their dreams that cause them to do this? Or is it because they are a perverse people? Will they say, "He has written it [the Koran] himself?" No! It is because they did not believe. If that is true, let them write a book like it.

The Meccans said that there was no Day of Doom. The Koran:

83:1 What! Do they believe that they will not be resurrected on the great day when all men will stand before the Lord of the worlds? Yes! The register [a record of actions] of the wicked is in Sidjin [a place in Hell where the sinners' records are kept]. And who will make you understand what Sidjin is? It is a complete record.

83:10 Woe on that day to those who deny Our signs, who regard the Judgment Day as a lie! No one regards it as a lie except the transgressor or the criminal, who, when Our signs are recited to him, says, "Old wives tales!" No! Their habits have become like rust on their hearts. Yes, they will be veiled from their Lord's light that day. Then they will be burned in Hell. They will be told, "This is what you called a lie."

83:18 No! But the register of the righteous is in Illiyoun [a place in Paradise where the actions of the righteous are recorded]. And who will make you understand what Illiyoun is? It is a complete record, attested to by the angels nearest Allah.

83:22 Surely, the righteous will live among delights! Seated on bridal couches they will gaze around. You will see the delight in their faces. Fine wines, sealed with musk, will be given them to drink. For those who have aspirations, aspire for wine mixed with the waters of Tasnim, a fountain where those close to Allah drink.

83:29 Sinners used to jeer at the believers and wink at one another when one passed by, and they jested as they returned to their own people. When they see believers, they say, "Those people have gone astray." And yet they were not sent to be the guardians of those people.

83:34 *On that day the faithful will mock the Kafirs, while they sit on bridal couches and watch them. Should not the Kafirs be paid back for what they did?*

1167 There was open hostility in the town. Quarrels increased, arguments got very heated. Complete disharmony dominated the town. The tribe started to abuse the recently converted Muslims.

1171 Many of the rich and powerful, who resisted Mohammed, earned their place in the Koran.

96:9 *What do you think of a man [Abu Jahl] who holds back a servant of Allah [Mohammed] when he prays? Do you think that he is on the right path, or practices piety? Do you think that he treats the truth as a lie and turns his back? Does he not know that Allah sees everything?*

96:15 *No! Certainly if he does not stop, We will grab him by the forelock [cutting off or holding by the forelock was a shame in Arabic culture], the lying, sinful forelock! Let him call his comrades [the other Meccans]. We will call the guards of Hell. No, do not obey him, rather, adore and get closer to Allah.*

111:1 *Let the hands of Abu Lahab [Mohammed's uncle and an opponent] die and let him die! His wealth and attainments will not help him. He will be burned in Hell, and his wife will carry the firewood, with a palm fiber rope around her neck.*

1178 In what would be very fortuitous for Mohammed, the Arabs of Medina were attracted to Mohammed's message. Since half of their town were Jews, the Arabs of Medina were used to the talk of only one god.

PUBLIC TEACHING

> 3:32 *Say: Obey Allah and His messenger, but if they reject it,*
> *then truly, Allah does not love those who reject the faith.*

The arguments continued. The Koran is filled with condemnation of the Meccans who argued with Mohammed.

> 25:32 *Those who disbelieve say, "Why was the Koran not revealed to him all at once?" It was revealed one part at a time so that We might strengthen your heart with it and so that We might rehearse it with you gradually, in slow, well-arranged stages.*
>
> 25:33 *They will not come to you with any difficult questions for which We have not provided you the true and best answers. Those who will be gathered together face down in Hell will have the worst place and will be the farthest away from the right path.*
>
> 18:56 *We do not send messengers except as bearers of glad tidings and to give warnings. Yet the Kafirs make false contentions so that they may refute the truth. They mock Our signs just like they do Our warnings. Who is more unjust than he who is reminded of His Lord's signs but turns away from them and forgets what His hands have done? Truly We have placed veils over their hearts so that they do not understand, and deafness over their ears. Even if you give them guidance, they will not follow.*

The Meccans called Mohammed crazy and mocked him.

> 37:12 *Truly you [Mohammed] are amazed when they mock. When they [the Meccans] are warned, they pay no attention. When they see a sign, they begin to mock and say, "This is obviously magic. What? Will we be resurrected after we are nothing but dust and bones? And what about our ancestors?"*
>
> 37:34 *Truly, that is how We deal with the guilty, because when they were told that there is no god but Allah, they swelled with pride and said, "Should we abandon our gods for a crazy poet?"*
>
> 37:37 *No! He [Mohammed] comes truthfully and confirms the prophets of old. You will surely taste the painful punishment, and you will be punished for what you have done, all except the sincere servants of Allah! They will have a fixed banquet of fruits; and they will be honored in the Garden of delight, facing one another on couches. A cup filled from a gushing*

spring will be passed among them, crystal clear and delicious to those who drink. It causes neither pain nor intoxication. And with them are companions [houris] with large eyes and modest glances, fair like a sheltered egg. They will ask one another questions. One of them will say, "I had a close friend who said, 'Are you one of those who accept the truth? What? When we have died, and become dust and bones, will we really be judged?'"

37:54 *He will say to those around him, "Will you look?" Looking down, he saw his friend in the depths of Hell. And he will say to him, "By Allah, you almost destroyed me. Except for my Lord's favor, I surely would have been one of those who came with you into torment."*

I183 Mohammed continued to preach the glory of Allah and condemn the Quraysh religion. He told them their way of life was wrong, their ancestors would burn in Hell, he cursed their gods, he despised their religion and divided the community, setting one tribesman against the others. The Quraysh felt that this was all past bearing. Tolerance had always been their way.

21:107 *We have sent you only to be a mercy for all people. Say: It has been revealed to me that Allah is the only god. Will you submit to Him? If they turn their backs, then say, "I have truthfully warned you alike. I do not know if Judgment Day will come sooner or later. Allah knows what is said openly and what you hide. I only know that you will be tried and that you may enjoy yourself for awhile." Say: My Lord judges with truth. Our Lord is the beneficent Allah Whose help is sought against lies you ascribe to Him.*

He continued to speak of Allah and the Koran. The Koran refers to itself many times and offers proofs of its truth.

67:16 *Are you confident that Allah in heaven will not open the earth and swallow you in an earthquake? Are you sure that Allah in heaven will not send a hurricane against you? You will understand My warning then! It is true that your ancestors rejected their prophets. Was not My wrath terrible?*

67:19 *Do they not see the birds above, spreading and folding their wings? Only merciful Allah could keep them aloft. He watches over everything.*

67:20 *Who could help you like an army except merciful Allah? The Kafirs are totally deluded. Who would provide for you if He withheld His provisions? Still, they continue to be proud and reject Him. Is the person groveling along on his face better than those who walk upright on a straight path?*

67:1 *Blessed is He whose hands hold the kingdom and has power over all things; Who created life and death to determine who conducts themselves best; and He is the mighty, the forgiving! He created and raised seven heavens, one above the other. You can not see one defect in merciful Allah's creation. Do you see a crack in the sky? Look again and again. Your vision will blur from looking, but you will find no defects.*

Here are other references in the Koran about the Koran:

Note: The first verse of most Koran chapters has words such as these two words—HA. MIM. No one knows their meaning or purpose.

44:1 *HA. MIM. By the book that makes everything clear!*
44:3 *We revealed it on a blessed night—because We are always warning man—on a night when every command is made clear by Our command. We are always sending Our messengers as a mercy from your Lord. He hears and knows everything.*

The Koran repeatedly says that Arabic is the true language of Allah.

20:112 *But those who believe and have done the right things will have no fear of wrong or loss. This is why We sent to you an Arabic Koran and explained in detail Our warnings so that they may fear Allah and heed them. Exalted above all is Allah, the King, the Truth! Do not hurry through its recital before its revelation is made complete to you. Instead say, "Lord, increase my knowledge."*
26:192 *This Book has come down from the Lord of the worlds. The faithful spirit [Gabriel] has come down with it upon your [Mohammed's] heart so that you may warn others in the clear Arabic language. Truly, it is foretold in the ancient scriptures. Is it not a sign that the learned men of the Israelites recognized? If We had revealed it to any of the non-Arabs and he had recited it to them, they would not have believed in it.*

Mohammed continued to make it clear that not believing the words he brought from Allah would lead to a violent and painful eternity.

76:4 *We have prepared chains, fetters, and a blazing fire for the Kafirs.*
76:5 *The righteous, however, will drink cups filled from a camphor fountain—the fountain Allah's servants drink from—as it flows from place to place rewarding those who perform their vows and fear a day whose evil will spread far and wide. Even when they were hungry they gave their food to the poor, the orphan, and the prisoner. "We feed you for Allah's sake. We are not looking for reward or thanks from you. We are afraid of suffering and punishment from Allah."*
76:11 *But Allah saved them from the evil of that day and brought them happiness and joy. He rewarded their patience with Paradise and silk*

robes. Reclining on couches, none will suffer from extreme heat or cold. Trees will shade them, and fruit will dangle near by. Silver cups and crystal goblets will pass among them: silver cups, transparent as glass, their size reflecting the measure of one's deeds. They will be given ginger-flavored wine from the fountain called Salsabil. They will be waited on by eternally young boys. When you look at them you would think they were scattered pearls. When you see it, you will see a vast kingdom of delights. They will wear richly brocaded green silk robes with silver bracelets on their arms, and they will quench their thirst with a pure drink given them by their Lord. This will be your reward. Your efforts will not go unnoticed. 76:23 We have sent the Koran to you in stages to be a revelation. Wait patiently for Allah's command, and do not obey the wicked and the unbelieving. Celebrate your Lord's name in the morning, in the evening, and at night. Adore him and praise him all night long.

76:27 But men love the fleeting present and ignore the dreadful day ahead. We have created them, and We built them strong. When We want to, We will make others to replace them. This is certainly a warning. Whoever chooses, will take a straight path to his Lord. But unless Allah wills it, because he is knowing and wise, you will not succeed. You will receive his mercy if he chooses to give it, but he has prepared a terrible punishment for the wicked.

Mecca was a small town and there were meetings about what to do about Mohammed.

43:79 Do they make plots against you? We also make plots. Do they think that We do not hear their secrets and their private conversations? We do, and Our messengers are there to record them.

38:1 SAD. I swear by the Koran, full of warning! Truly, the Kafirs must be filled with arrogant pride to oppose you. How many earlier generations did We destroy? In the end, they cried for mercy when there was no time to escape!

38:4 They are skeptical that a messenger would come to them from their own people, and the Kafirs say, "This man is a sorcerer and a liar! Has he combined all the gods into one Allah? That is an amazing thing!" And their chiefs [the leaders of the opposition to Mohammed in Mecca] went about and said, "Walk away. Remain faithful to your gods. This is a plot. We have never heard of such a thing in the earlier religion. This is nothing but an invented tale!"

38:8 They say, "Why, of all people, has the message been sent to him [Mohammed]?" Yes! They doubt My warnings because they have not tasted My vengeance. Do they possess the blessings of the mighty, your Lord's mercy? Is the kingdom of the heavens and the earth and everything in between in their hands? If so, let them climb up to the heavens if they can! Any allies [Mohammed's opponents] remaining here will be defeated.

MORE ARGUMENTS WITH THE MECCANS

I188, 189 One of the Quraysh said, "Well, if you speak for and represent the only true god, then perhaps his Allah could do something for them."

"This land is dry. Let his Allah send them a river next to Mecca."

"They were cramped being next to the mountains. Let his Allah open up some space by moving the mountains back."

"Our best members are dead. Let your Allah renew them to life and in particular send back the best leader of our tribe, Qusayy. We will ask Qusayy whether or not you speak truly."

I189 Mohammed said that he was sent as a messenger, not to do such work. They could either accept his message or reject it and be subject to the loss. Then one of them said, "If you won't use your Allah to help us, then let your Allah help you. Send an angel to confirm you and prove to us that we are wrong. As long as the angel was present, let him make Mohammed wealthy, we will know that you represent Allah and we are wrong." The Quraysh wanted miracles as a proof.

> 15:4 *We never destroy a city whose term was not preordained. No nation can delay or change its destiny. They say: "You [Mohammed] to whom the message was revealed, you are surely insane. If you were telling the truth, why did you not bring angels to us?"*
> 15:8 *We do not send the angels without good reason. If We did, the Kafirs would still not understand. Surely, We have sent down the message, and surely, We will guard it. Before your time, We sent apostles to the sects of the ancient peoples, but they mocked every messenger. Similarly, We allow doubt to enter the hearts of the sinners. They do not believe it, even though the example of the ancients has preceded them. Even if We opened a gate into heaven for them the entire time they ascended, they would say, "Our eyes are playing tricks on us. No, we are bewitched."*

I189 Mohammed did not perform miracles, because such things were not what Allah had appointed him to do.

I189 They then said, "Did not your Lord know that we would ask you these questions? Then your Lord could have prepared you with better answers. And your Lord could have told you what to tell us if we don't believe. We hear that you are getting this Koran from a man named Al Rahman from another town. We don't believe in Al Rahman. Our conscience is clear. We must either destroy you or you must destroy us. Bring your angels and we will believe them."

26:204 *What! Do they seek to hasten Our punishment? What do you think? If after giving them their fill for years and their punishment finally comes upon them, how will their pleasures help them? We have never destroyed a city that We did not warn first with a reminder. We did not treat them unjustly.*

26:210 *The devils were not sent down with the Koran. It does not suit them, and they do not have the power because they are banned from hearing it. Do not call upon any god but Allah, or you will be doomed. Rather, warn your close relatives,*

26:215 *And be kind to the believers who follow you. If they disobey you, say, "I will not be responsible for your actions." Put your trust in Him who is mighty and merciful, Who sees you when you stand in prayer, and your demeanor among the worshipers, because He hears and knows everything.*

I191 Mohammed would come to the Kabah and tell the Meccans what terrible punishments that Allah had delivered to the others in history who had not believed their prophets. That was now one of his constant themes. Allah destroyed others like you who did not listen to men like me.

36:1 *YA. SIN. I swear by the wise Koran that you are surely one of the messengers on a straight path, a revelation of the mighty, the merciful, sent to warn a people whose fathers were not warned, and consequently remain heedless.*

36:7 *Our sentence against them is just because they do not believe. We have bound their necks with chains that reach the chin, forcing their heads up. We have placed barriers in front, behind, and over them, so they can not see. It does not matter whether you warn them or not, because they will not believe. You can only warn those who follow the message and fear merciful Allah in private. Give them glad tidings of forgiveness and a generous reward. It is true We will give life to the dead and that We record what they will do and what they have done. We have recorded everything in Our perfect ledger.*

According to the Koran the ancient towns of Arabia were destroyed because they did not believe their prophet.

26:141 *The people of Thamud [the people of a ruined Nabatean city near Medina] rejected the messengers. Their brother Salih said to them, "Will you not fear Allah? I am a faithful messenger worthy of all trust. Fear Allah and obey me. I ask for no reward. My reward comes only from the Lord of the worlds. Will you be left safely to enjoy all you have among gardens and fountains and corn-fields and palm-trees, heavy with fruit, and—insolent as you are—your homes carved from the mountain stone?*

Fear Allah and obey me. Do not obey the bidding of the extravagant who make mischief in the land, and do not reform."

27:45 *Long ago We sent to the Thamud their brother Salih saying, "Worship Allah." But they became two quarreling factions. He said, "My people, why do you embrace evil, rather than good? Why do you not ask Allah's forgiveness so that you may receive mercy?"*
27:47 *They said, "We predict that you and your followers will bring us evil." He said, "The evil that you sense will befall you, will come from Allah. You are a people on trial."*
27:48 *In the city there were nine men from one family who made mischief in the land and would not reform. They said, "Swear to one another by Allah that we will attack Salih and his family at night, and we will tell his vengeance-seeking heirs that we did not see the murder of his family, and we will be telling the truth." They plotted and planned, but We also plotted, even though they did not realize. See how their plotting turned out. We destroyed them and their entire people. You may still see their ruined homes which were destroyed because they were wicked. Surely this is a sign for those who understand. We saved those who believed and acted righteously.*

The Koran of Mecca reworks the Jewish stories for Mohammed's benefit. Here are stories about David, a king of the Jews:

38: 17 *Be patient with what they say, and remember Our servant David, a powerful man, who always looked repentantly to Allah. We made the mountains sing the praises of Allah in unison with him in the morning and the evening, and the birds gathered together; all joined him in praise of Allah. We made his kingdom strong and gave him wisdom and sound Judgment.*
38:21 *Have you heard the story of the two disputing men who climbed the wall of David's private chamber? David was frightened when they entered his room. They said, "Do not be afraid. We have a dispute, and one of us has certainly wronged the other. Judge where the truth lies between us, and do not be unjust, but guide us to the right way. My brother has ninety-nine ewes [female sheep], and I have only one. He pressured me and said, 'Let me have her.'"*
38:24 *David replied, "Certainly he has wronged you by insisting that you give him your ewe. It is true that many partners wrong one another the exception being those who believe and behave correctly. There are few of those." David realized that We had tried him. He asked forgiveness from his Lord, fell down bowing, and repented.*
38:25 *So We forgave him this sin; truly he is honored and well received by Us and has an excellent place in Paradise. It was said to him, "David, We have indeed made you a vice-regent on earth. Use truth and justice when judging between men, and do not follow your passions because they*

may cause you to stray from Allah's path. Those who stray from Allah's path will meet a terrible punishment because they have forgotten the Judgment Day.

Noah is considered to be a prophet in Islam.

71:1 *We sent Noah to his people and said to him, "Warn your people before a terrible punishment befalls them." He said, "My people, I come to you as a plain-speaking warner. Serve and fear Allah and obey me. He will forgive you your sins and give you respite until the appointed time, because when Allah's appointed time has come, it can not be delayed. If only you knew this!"*

71:5 *He said, "Lord, I have cried to my people day and night; and my cries only increase their aversion. Whenever I cry to them so that you may forgive them, they cover their ears and cover themselves in their cloaks, and persist stubbornly in their error. Then I called loudly to them. Then I spoke plainly, and I spoke to them privately and I said, 'Beg your Lord for forgiveness because he is ready to forgive. He will open the sky and send down rain in abundance. He will increase your wealth and children and will give you gardens and rivers. What is the matter with you that you refuse to seek goodness from Allah's hand when it was Him who made you in diverse stages?'"*

71:15 *"Do you not see how Allah created the seven heavens and set them one above another? He placed the moon there and made it a light, and made the sun a lamp and placed it there, and Allah caused you to spring out of the earth like a plant. Later he will turn you back into the earth and bring you out again. Allah has spread the earth for you like a carpet so that you may walk there along spacious paths." Noah said, "Lord, they rebel against me and follow those whose wealth and children add only to their troubles."*

71:22 *And they devised a great plot. They said, "Do not forsake your gods; do not forsake Wadd, or Sowah, or Yaghuth nor Yahuk or Nesr [names of Semitic gods]." They have led many astray and have added only error to the ways of the wicked. Because of their sins, they were drowned and forced into the fire, and they discovered that Allah was their only shelter.*

71:26 *And Noah said, "Lord, do not leave one family of Kafirs alive on earth. Because if you do, then they will trick your servants and will only breed more sinners and Kafirs. Lord, forgive me and my parents and every believer that enters my house and all the male and female believers. Give nothing but destruction to the wicked."*

Here are other Jewish references:

38:41 *Do you remember Our servant Job when he cried to his Lord, "Satan has afflicted me with distress and torment." We said to him, "Stamp the*

21

ground with your foot. Here is a spring, a cool washing place, and water to drink." And We gave him back his family and doubled their number as an example of Our mercy and as a reminder for men of understanding. We said to him, "Take up in your hand a branch and strike her with it, and do not break your oath.¹" Truly, We found him to be full of patience and constant. He was an excellent servant, because he constantly turned toward Us in repentance.

38:45 *And remember Our servants Abraham, Isaac, and Jacob, men of power and vision. Surely We purified and chose them for a special purpose, proclaiming the message of the afterlife. They were, in Our eyes, truly some of the select and the good.*

38:48 *And remember Ishmael, Elisha, and Zul-Kifl [Ezekiel]: all of them belong among the chosen.*

38:49 *This is a reminder, and, surely, the righteous will have an excellent home in the afterlife, the Gardens of Eternity whose doors will always be open for them. They can recline and call at their leisure for abundant fruit and drink. They will have virgins of their own age, who glance modestly. This is what you are promised on the Judgment Day. This is Our gift to you. It will never fail.*

Abraham

37:83 *Truly, Abraham shared this faith when he brought a perfect heart to his Lord and he said to his father and to his people, "What are you worshiping? A lie! Do you want gods besides Allah? And what do you think about the Lord of the worlds?"*

37:88 *Then he looked up and gazed at the stars and said, "Truly, I am ill." [Abraham's peoples' worship involved the stars] And they turned their backs on him and left. He turned to the images of their gods and said, "Do you not eat? What is wrong with you? Why do you not speak?" He began to attack them, striking them with his right hand.*

37:94 *As his tribesmen came running back to him, he said, "Do you worship what you have carved when Allah has created you and what you make?" They said, "Build a pyre for him, and throw him into the blazing fire." They tried to plot against him, but We spoiled their plans. And Abraham said, "Truly, I will go to my Lord, and he will guide me. Oh Lord, give me a righteous son." We gave him the good news of a gentle son.*

37:102 *When the son [Ishmael] grew tall enough to work, his father said to him, "Son, a dream tells me that I should sacrifice you. What do you think?" He said, "Father, do what you are commanded. If Allah wills, you will find me patient."*

---

1. Job swore to beat his wife with one hundred blows. Later he softened, and, to fulfill his oath, he put one hundred small twigs in his hand and hit her once.

37:103 *After they had surrendered themselves to the will of Allah, he laid his son [Ishmael] face down. We cried out to him, "Abraham! You have satisfied the vision." See how We reward the righteous. This was obviously a clear test. And We ransomed his son with an impressive victim [a ram], and We left this for him to be honored through posterity.*

37:109 *"Peace be on Abraham!" This is how We reward the good, because he was one of Our believing servants.*

37:112 *And We gave him the good news of the birth of Isaac—a righteous prophet—We bestowed Our blessing on him and Isaac. Among their descendants [the Jews] are some that do good and others that do harm to their souls.*

A Moses story:

20:9 *Have you heard the story of Moses? He saw a fire and said to his family, "Wait here. I see a fire. Maybe I can bring an ember from it, or find a guide there."*

20:11 *When he came to it, a voice called out, "Moses! I am your Lord. Take off your shoes. You are in the sacred Tuwa valley. I have chosen you. Listen to what I say. I am Allah. There is no god but Me. Worship Me and observe prayer to celebrate My praise. The Hour [Judgment Day] is certainly coming. I plan to keep it a secret so that all souls may be rewarded for their actions. Therefore do not let those who disbelieve and follow their lusts turn you away from the truth and cause your destruction.*

20:17 *What is that in your right hand, Moses?" He said, "It is my staff. I lean on it and beat the leaves down with it for my sheep, among other things." Allah said, "Throw it down, Moses!" He threw it down, and it turned into a slithering serpent. Allah said, "Grab it and do not be afraid. We will change it back to its former state. Now put your hand under your arm. It will come out white [with leprosy], but unhurt. Another sign so that We may show you Our greatest signs. Go to Pharaoh, because he has exceeded all limits."*

20:25 *Moses said, "My Lord, relieve my mind and make my task easy. Untie my tongue so they can understand what I say. Give me an assistant from my family—Aaron, my brother—add his strength to mine, and make him share my task. We will glorify you without pause, because you are always watching." He said, "Moses, your request is granted. We have shown you favor before. Our message to your mother inspired her saying: 'Put him into a chest and throw it in the river; the river will leave him on the bank where he will be found by an enemy to Me and to him.' But I cast my love down upon you so that you might be raised under my eye."*

20:46 *He said, "Do not be afraid, because I am with the both of you. I will listen and watch over you. Go to him and say, 'Surely we have been sent by your Lord. Let the Children of Israel go with us and do not torment them.*

We bring you a sign from your Lord, and peace to him who follows His guidance. It has been revealed to us that those who reject him and turn away will be punished."

20:49 *And Pharaoh said, "Who is your Lord, Moses?"*

20:50 *Moses said, "Our Lord is the One who created everything and gave it all purpose."*

20:77 *We revealed to Moses, "Take away My servants and travel by night. Cleave a dry path through the sea for them. Do not be afraid of being overtaken and have no fear." Pharaoh and his army followed, but the sea overwhelmed them, because he misled his people by not guiding them.*

20:80 *Children of Israel! We saved you from your enemies, and We made a pact with you on the sacred side of the mountain and sent down to you manna and quails. We said, "Eat the good things that We have given you, but not to excess, or My wrath may fall on you, and whoever My wrath falls upon will surely perish. I will surely forgive him who turns to Allah and believes and does good deeds, and listens to guidance."*

I192 Since Mohammed and the Koran claimed Jewish roots, the Quraysh decided to send their story teller to the Jews in Medina and ask for help. The Rabbis said, "Ask him these three questions. If he knows the answer then he is a prophet, if not then he is a fake."

"What happened to the young men who disappeared in ancient days."

"Ask him about the mighty traveler who reached the ends of the East and the West."

"Ask him, What is the spirit?"

I192 The Koran answered all the questions and statements of the Quraysh. With regards to the question about what happened to the young men in ancient times:

18:9 *Do you believe that the Sleepers of the Cave and the Inscription [an unknown reference] were among Our signs? When the youths [the Sleepers] took refuge in the cave, they said, "Lord, give us Your mercy and cause us to act rightly." We drew a veil over them depriving them of their senses for many years. Then We roused them so that We could know which would best determine the number of years they lived in the cave.*
[...]
18:25 *They remained in their cave for three hundred years, though some say three hundred and nine. Say: Allah knows exactly how long they stayed. He knows the secrets of the heavens and the earth. Man has no guardian besides Him. He does not allow any to share His power.*

As to the question about the mighty traveler (the Koran considers Alexander, the Great to be a prophet:

> 18:83 *They will ask you about Zul-Qarnain [Alexander, the Great]. Say: I will recite to you an account of him. We established his power in the land and gave him the means to achieve any of his aims. So he followed a path, until, when he reached the setting of the sun, he found it setting in a muddy pond. Near by he found a people. We said, "Zul-Qarnain, you have the authority to either punish them or to show them kindness."*
> 18:87 *He said, "Whoever does wrong, we will certainly punish. Then he will be returned to his Lord, Who will punish him with a terrible punishment. But whoever believes and does good deeds shall be given a wonderful reward, and We will give them easy commands to obey."*

The question—what is the spirit?

> 17:85 *They will ask you about the spirit [probably the angel Gabriel]. Say: The spirit is commanded by my Lord, and you are given only a little knowledge about it. If We wished, We could take Our revelations away from you. Then you would find no one to intercede with us on your behalf except as a mercy from your Lord. Surely His kindness to you is great.*

The Quraysh had questions about proof of Mohammed's messages. Here is the Koran's restatement of their questions about angels coming, creating rivers, creating wealth and any other miracle to prove Mohammed's validity. The Koran's response:

> 17:88 *Say: If men and jinn were assembled to produce something like this Koran, they could not produce its equal, even though they assisted each other. And certainly in this Koran We have explained to man every kind of argument, and yet most men refuse everything except disbelief. They [the Meccans] say, "We will not believe in you until you cause a spring to gush forth from the earth for us; or until you have a garden of date trees and grape vines, and cause rivers to gush abundantly in their midst; or when you cause the sky to fall down in pieces, as you claim will happen; or when you bring us face-to-face with Allah and the angels; or when you have a house of gold; or when you ascend into heaven; and even then we will not believe in your ascension until you bring down a book for us which we may read." Say: Glory be to my Lord! Am I nothing except a man, a messenger?*
> 17:94 *What keeps men from believing when guidance has come to them but that they say, "Has Allah sent a man like us to be His messenger?" Say: If angels walked the earth, We would have sent down from heaven an angel as Our messenger. Say: Allah is a sufficient witness between you and me. He is well acquainted with His servants and He sees everything.*

17:97 *Whoever Allah guides, he is a follower of the right way, and whoever He causes to err, they shall not find any to assist them but Him. We will gather them together on the Resurrection Day, face down, blind, deaf, and dumb. Hell will be their home. Every time its flames die down, We will add fuel to the Fire. This is their reward because they did not believe Our signs and said, "When we are reduced to bones and dust, will we really be raised up as a new creation?"*

This is the Koran's answer to the Kafirs who said that the Koran was a lie based on old stories:

25:3 *Still they have worshiped other gods, besides Him, who have created nothing and were themselves created. They are powerless to work good or evil for themselves, nor can they control life or death or resurrection. But the Kafirs say, "This [the Koran] is nothing but a lie which he [Mohammed] has created with the assistance of others producing slander and injustice."*
25:5 *They say, " These are ancient fables that he has written down. They are dictated to him morning and night."*
25:6 *Say: The Koran was revealed by Him who knows the secrets of the heavens and the earth. He is truly forgiving and merciful.*

I204 When Mohammed called upon Meccans to submit to Islam, they said, "Our hearts are veiled; we don't understand what you say. There is something in our ears so we can't hear you."

The Koranic response:

17:45 *When you recite the Koran, We place an invisible barrier between you and the Kafirs. We place veils over their hearts and deafness in their ears so that they do not understand it, and when you mention only your Lord, Allah, in the Koran, they turn their backs and flee from the truth. We know absolutely what they listen to when they listen to you, and when they speak privately, the wicked say, "You follow a mad man!" See what they compare you to. But they have gone astray and cannot find the way.*

Mohammed's opponents are frequently quoted and paraphrased:

43:29 *I have allowed these men and their fathers to enjoy the pleasurable things of this life until the truth comes to them and a messenger makes things clear.*
43:30 *But when the truth came to them, they said: "This is trickery, and we reject it." And they say, "Why was this Koran not revealed to a great man of one of the two cities [Mecca and Taif]?"*

21:1 *Man's final reckoning draws ever closer to him, and yet he heedlessly continues to turn away. Every new warning that comes to him from his Lord is ridiculed. The wicked confer secretly and say, "Is he a man like you, or something more? Will you succumb to witchcraft with your eyes wide open?"*

21:4 *Say: My Lord knows what is spoken in the heavens and on earth. He is the hearer and the knower of all things.*

21:5 *They say, "No, This is nothing but jumbled dreams. He made it up. He is just a crazy poet! We want him to bring us a sign similar to those given to the prophets of the past!" Up to their time, despite Our warnings, not a single city that We destroyed believed. Will these people believe?*

Now verses in the Koran began to form the basis of the legal system (the Sharia) of Islam.

17:31 *Do not kill your children because you fear poverty. We will provide for them as well as for you. Surely, killing them is a terrible sin.*

17:32 *Have nothing to do with adultery. It is a shameful act and an evil path that leads to other evils.*

17:33 *Do not kill any one whom Allah has forbidden to be slain [a Muslim] unless it is for a just cause [apostasy, retribution for a killing]. Whoever is unjustly slain, We have given their heirs the authority to either forgive or demand retribution, but do not allow him to exceed limits in slaying because he will be helped by the law.*

STRUGGLES

CHAPTER 3

> 8:20 *Believers! Be obedient to Allah and His messenger, and
> do not turn your backs now that you know the truth. Do
> not be like the ones who say, "We hear," but do not obey.*

I217 Each of the clans of the Quraysh began to persecute those Muslims that they had any power over. The Meccans did not believe Mohammed.

> 34:43 *For when Our clear signs are recited to them, they say, "This is merely a man who would turn you away from your father's religion." They say, "This (Koran) is only a lie." And when they hear the truth, the Kafirs say, "This is nothing but clear sorcery." Yet We did not give them any books to study deeply, nor have We sent them a messenger with warnings. Those before them rejected the truth, but they have not given Us a tenth of what We have given to them. When they rejected My messengers, My vengeance was terrible.*
>
> 34:46 *Say: I advise you in one thing: that you stand up before Allah and reflect. There is no madness in your fellow citizen [Mohammed]. He is only your warner before a severe punishment.*

This verse allows a Muslim to avoid being persecuted about his religion. A Muslim may cover true beliefs about Islam to a Kafir.

> 3:28 *Say: Whether you hide what is in your hearts or make it widely known, Allah knows all. He knows all that is in the heavens and earth. Allah has control over all things.*

I235 A story teller boasted that he could tell better old stories and would tell them in competition with Mohammed. But the story teller was an Kafir and the Koran condemned him, as well as all Kafirs.

> 31:6 *There are men who engage in idle tales [A Persian story-teller in Mecca said that his stories were better than Mohammed's] without knowing, and they mislead others from the way of Allah and turn it to scorn. There will be a shameful punishment for them. When Our signs are revealed to him, he turns away in arrogance as if he had not heard them, as though there were deafness in his ears. Give him tidings of a terrible punishment. Those who will believe and do good works, will enjoy the Gardens of Bliss, where they will abide forever. It is Allah's true promise, and He is mighty and wise.*

31:10 *He created the heavens without pillars that can be seen and put mountains firmly on the earth so that they would not move. He scattered over it animals of every sort. He sent down rain from the heavens and caused every kind of noble plant to grow. This is the creation of Allah. Now show me what others beside Him have created. The wrongdoers are in obvious error.*

The Koran describes the qualities of Allah.

40:61 *Allah made the night so you could rest and the day to give you light for seeing. Allah is rich in bounties to men, but most men do not give thanks. Such is Allah your Lord, creator of all things. There is no god but Allah. Why then are you turned from the truth? Those who deny the signs of Allah are turned aside.*

40:64 *Allah made the earth for you as a resting place and built up the heavens over it. He formed you and made your forms beautiful, and provided you with good things. This is Allah your Lord. Blessed be Allah, Lord of the worlds. He is the living one. There is no god but Allah. Call on Him with sincere devotion. Praise be to Allah, Lord of the worlds.*

40:66 *Say: I am forbidden to worship any beside Allah after the clear signs that have come to me from my Lord, and I am commanded to submit to the Lord of the worlds.*

THE SATANIC VERSES

Mohammed was always thinking of how he could persuade all the Meccans. It came to him that the three gods of the Quraysh could intercede with Allah. Mohammed said, "These are the exalted high flying cranes whose intercession is approved." The Meccans were delighted and happy. Satan had fooled Mohammed.

22:52 *Never have We sent a prophet or messenger before you whom Satan did not tempt with evil desires, but Allah will bring Satan's temptations to nothing. Allah will affirm His revelations, for He is knowing and wise. He makes Satan's suggestions a temptation for those whose hearts are diseased or for those whose hearts are hardened. Truly, this is why the Kafirs are in great opposition so that those who have been given knowledge will know that the Koran is the truth from their Lord and so that they may believe in it and humbly submit to Him. Allah will truly guide the believers to the right path.*

22:55 *But the Kafirs will never stop doubting until the Hour of Judgment comes upon them unaware or until the punishment of a disastrous day. On that day Allah's rule will be absolute. He will judge between them. And those who believed and did good works will be led into Gardens of delight.*

As for the Kafirs who treated Our signs as lies, they will receive a shameful punishment.

The Koran is constant in its admonitions about whom a Muslim should be friends with (there are 12 verses that say a Muslim is not the friend of a Kafir.

9:23 *Oh, Believers, do not make friends of your fathers or your brothers if they love unbelief above Islam. He who makes them his friends does wrong. Say: If your fathers, and your sons, and your brothers, and your wives, and your kin-folks, and the wealth which you have gained, and the merchandise that you fear you will not sell, and the dwellings in which you delight—if all are dearer to you than Allah and His Messenger and efforts on His Path, then wait until Allah's command comes to pass. Allah does not guide the impious.*

3:28 *Believers should not take Kafirs as friends in preference to other believers. Those who do this will have none of Allah's protection and will only have themselves as guards. Allah warns you to fear Him for all will return to Him.*

3:118 *Believers! Do not become friends with anyone except your own people. The Kafirs will not rest until they have corrupted you. They wish nothing but your ruin. Their hatred of you is made clear by their words, but even greater hatred is hidden within their hearts. We have made Our signs clear to you. Therefore, do your best to comprehend them.*

5:57 *Oh, you who believe, do not take those who have received the Scriptures [Jews and Christians] before you, who have scoffed and jested at your religion, or who are Kafirs for your friends. Fear Allah if you are true believers. When you call to prayer, they make it a mockery and a joke. This is because they are a people who do not understand.*

I260 In the market there was a Christian slave who ran a booth. Mohammed would go and speak with him at length. This led to the Quraysh saying that what Mohammed said in the Koran, came from the Christian slave. The Koran's response:

32:1 *ALIF. LAM. MIM. This Book is without a doubt a revelation sent down from the Lord of the worlds. Do they say, "He [Mohammed] has made it up"? No. It is the truth sent from your Lord so that you may warn a people who have not yet been warned so that they may be guided.*

THE NIGHT JOURNEY

17:1 *Glory to Allah, Who took His servant on a night time journey from the Sacred Mosque in Mecca to the furthest Mosque, whose neighborhood*

We have blessed so that We might show him Our signs: He, and only He, hears and sees all things.

1264 Gabriel took Mohammed to the farthest mosque. There Jesus, Abraham, Moses, and other prophets. Mohammed led them in prayer. Then Gabriel took Mohammed up to the seven heavens.

1271 When Mohammed got to the seventh heaven his Lord gave him the duty of fifty prayers a day. When he returned, Moses asked him how many prayers Allah had given him. When Moses heard that it was fifty, he said, "Prayer is a weighty matter and your people are weak. Go back and ask your Lord to reduce the number for you and your community. Allah reduced the number to five. In the Night Journey we see Mohammed as the successor to the Jewish prophets.

Here we see the story of Noah and Moses adapted to Mohammed's needs.

10:71 *Tell them the history of Noah when he said to his people, "Oh, my people, if my stay and my reminding you of the signs of Allah are grievous to you, I still trust Allah. So choose a course of action—you and your false gods. Do not let your plans be uncertain to you. Then come to some decision about me, and do not delay. If you turn your backs on me, I ask no reward from you. My reward is with Allah alone, and I am commanded to submit to Allah's will." But they treated him as a liar, and We rescued him and those with him in the ark, and We made them to inherit the earth while We drowned those who rejected Our signs. See what was the end of those who were warned?*

10:74 *Then after him, We sent messengers to their peoples, and they brought them clear signs, but they would not believe in what they had denied earlier. So We seal up the hearts of the transgressors. After them We sent Moses and Aaron with Our signs to Pharaoh and his nobles, but they were arrogant and a guilty people. When the truth came to them from Us, they said, "This is clear sorcery."*

10:77 *Moses said, "What do you say of the truth when it has come to you, 'Is this sorcery?' but sorcerers will not prosper."*

10:78 *They said, "Have you come to us to turn us away from the faith of our fathers so that you and your brother will have greatness in this land? We are not going to believe in you."*

10:79 *Pharaoh said, "Fetch me every skilled magician." When the magicians arrived, Moses said to them, "Cast down what you have to cast."*

10:81 *And when they had cast them down, Moses said, "What you have brought is sorcery, and Allah will render them vain. Allah does not uphold the work of mischief-makers. Allah will verify the truth by his words, though the guilty may be averse to it." And none believed in Moses except some of the children of his people because they feared that Pharaoh and his*

31

nobles would persecute them. Pharaoh was a tyrant in the land and one who committed excesses.

10:84 And Moses said, "Oh, my people, if you believe in Allah, put your trust in Him and submit."

10:85 They said, "In Allah we put our trust. Oh, our Lord, do not make us subject to the persecution of unjust people, and deliver us by Your mercy from the unbelieving people."

Islam defines the Jews.

45:16 Long ago we gave to the Children of Israel the Torah and the wisdom and the gift of prophecy, and We provided them with the good things. We favored them over all nations. We gave them clear commandments, but after they received knowledge, they began to differ amongst themselves because of envy. Your Lord will judge between them on the Day of Reckoning concerning these issues which separated them.

7:163 Ask them about the town that stood by the sea, how the Jews broke the Sabbath. Their fish came to them on their Sabbath day appearing on the surface of the water. But during the work week there were no fish to catch. So We made a trial of them for they were evildoers. And when some of them said, "Why do you preach to those whom Allah is about to destroy or chastise with awful doom?" They said, "To do our duty for the Lord so that they may be able to ward off evil."

7:165 When they disregarded the warnings that had been given to them [not to work on the Sabbath], We rescued those who had forbidden wrongdoing, and We punished the wrongdoers for their transgressions. But when they persisted in what they had been forbidden, We said to them, "Be as apes, despised and loathed." [The Jews were changed into apes.]

7:167 Then the Lord declared that until Resurrection Day, He would use others to punish the Jews, for the Lord is quick to punish, and most surely is He forgiving and merciful. And We sent them out on the land as separate nations. Some of them were righteous and some were not. We have tried them with prosperity and adversity in order that they might return to Us.

I272 Mohammed continued to preach Islam and condemn the old Arabic religions. There were those of the Quraysh who defended their culture and religion and argued with him. Mohammed called them mockers and cursed one of them, "Oh Allah, blind him and kill his son." The Koran records the Meccan's resistance as plots and schemes.

6:124 So We have placed wicked ringleaders in every city to scheme there, but they only plot against themselves, and they do not realize it. And when a sign comes to them they say, "We will not believe until we receive one like those that Allah's messengers received." Allah knows best where to place His message. The Kafirs will be disgraced when they receive their punishment for their scheming.

6:125 *For those whom Allah intends to guide, He will open their hearts to Islam. But for those whom He intends to mislead, He will make their hearts closed and hard, as though they had to climb up to the heavens. Thus does Allah penalize the Kafirs. And this is the right way of your Lord. We have detailed Our signs for those who will listen and see. They shall have an abode of peace with their Lord. He will be their protecting friend because of their works.*

And if Mohammed were actually a prophet, why not show them something other than words. Why not do a miracle?

13:27 *The Kafirs say: Why does his Lord not send a sign down to him? Say: Allah will truly mislead whom he chooses and will guide to Himself those who turn to Him. They believe and their hearts find rest in remembering Allah. Without a doubt all hearts find rest in the remembrance of Allah. Those who believe and do what is right will be blessed and find joy in the end.*

13:30 *Therefore, We have sent you to a nation before which other nations have passed away so that you may recite Our revelations to them. Nevertheless they deny the merciful Allah. Say: He is my Lord; there is no god but Him. I put my trust in Him, and to Him I will return.*

13:31 *If there were a Koran that could move mountains, tear the earth apart, or make the dead speak, this would be it! Allah is in command of all things! Do the believers not know that if it had been Allah's will, He could have guided all the people? Disaster will never cease to afflict the Kafirs for their wrongful deeds or to come into their homes until Allah's will is fulfilled. Allah will not fail to keep His promise.*

13:32 *Many messengers who came before you were mocked. For a long time We allowed the Kafirs to go unpunished, but finally We punished them. Then how terrible was Our punishment!*

If Judgment Day were to come, then the Meccans asked Mohammed to tell Allah to bring it here this day and prove Mohammed was a true prophet.

29:44 *Allah created the heavens and the earth in truth. This is a sign to those who believe.*

29:47 *So it is that We have sent down the Book [Koran] to you [Mohammed]. Those [the Jews] to whom We have given the Book of the law believe in it, and some other Arabians there believe in it. None, save the Kafirs, reject our signs.*

29:48 *You [Mohammed] were not a reader of the Scripture before this book came, nor did you write one with your right hand. Then the critics could have treated it as a vain thing and doubted it. But it is a clear sign in the hearts of those whom knowledge has reached. None but the unjust reject Our signs. They say, "Why are the signs not sent down to him from his Lord?" Say: The signs are in the power of Allah alone. I am only a plain warner. Is it not enough for them that We have revealed to you the Book to be recited to them? This is a mercy and a warning to those who believe. Say: Allah is witness enough between me and you. He knows all that is in the heavens and the earth. Those who believe in the falsehood and reject Allah—these will be the lost ones.*

29:53 They will challenge you to hasten the punishment. If there had not been a season fixed for it, the punishment would have already come upon them. It will come on them suddenly when they are not looking for it. They will ask you to hasten the punishment, but Hell will encompass the Kafirs. One day the punishment shall wrap around them, both from above them and from below them, and Allah will say, "Taste your own doings."

29:56 Oh, My servants who believe, My earth is vast; therefore, serve Me. Every soul will have a taste of death. Then to Us you will return. Those who believe and serve righteousness, We will house in Gardens with palaces, beneath which the rivers flow. They will abide there forever. How good the reward of the workers, those who patiently endure and put their trust in their Lord.

Mohammed continued to tell about older Arabian cultures that had refused to listen to their prophets. In every case, Allah smote them with a terrible scourge.

41:13 But if they turn away, say to them, "I have warned you of a disaster like the scourge that punished Ad [Ad lay on an old trade route north of Mecca. It was abandoned in Mohammed's day] and Thamud [the people of a ruined Nabatean city near Medina]."

41:14 When their messengers came from all directions saying, "Serve only Allah," they answered, "If our Lord had wished, He would have sent angels down to us, so we do not believe the message you carry."

41:15 As for the people of Ad, they were unjustly arrogant throughout the land, and they said, "Who has more power than us?" Could they not see that Allah, Who created them, was more powerful than themselves? Still, they continued to reject Our signs! So we sent a furious wind against them during days of disaster so that We might make them taste the penalty of disgrace in this life. The penalty of the afterlife will be even more disgraceful. They will not be helped.

41:17 We showed the people of Thamud [the people of a ruined Nabatean city near Medina] the right way, but they preferred blindness to guidance. So the scourge of humiliation overtook them because that was what they earned. However, We saved those who believed and acted righteously. On the day when the enemies of Allah are gathered to face the Fire, they will be marched together in groups. When they reach the Fire, their ears, eyes, and skin will bear witness against them for what they have done.

41:21 They will say to their skins, "Why do you testify against us?" And their reply will be, "Allah, Who has given speech to all things, has made us speak. He created you originally, and you will be returned to Him. You did not try to hide yourselves so that your ears, eyes, and skins could testify against you. You thought that Allah was unaware of most of the things that you did. But this evil thought of yours [that there are other gods] has brought you to destruction, and now you are one of the lost."

41:24 And though they are resigned, the Fire will still be their home. If they ask for goodwill, they will not receive it. We have given them companions in this world who made their present and past seem good to them. They deserve the fate of the past generations of jinns and men. They are certainly losers.

MOHAMMED'S PROTECTOR AND WIFE BOTH DIE

I278 After Abu Talib's death, the pressure on Mohammed grew. It reached the point where one of the Quraysh threw dust at Mohammed. This was the worst that happened.

The death of his wife, Khadija, had no political effect, but it was a blow to Mohammed. His wife was his chief confidant, and she consoled him.

MOHAMMED'S NEW MARRIAGES

About three months after the death of Khadija Mohammed married Sauda, a widow and a Muslim.

Abu Bakr had a daughter, Aisha, who was six years old. Soon after marrying Sauda Mohammed was betrothed to Aisha, who was to become his favorite wife. The consummation would not take place until she turned nine.

POLITICAL BEGINNINGS

CHAPTER 4

*24:52 It is such as obey Allah and His Apostle, and fear
Allah and do right, that will win (in the end).*

I279 With his protector's death, Mohammed needed political allies. Mohammed went to the city of Taif, about fifty miles away. In Taif he met with three brothers who were politically powerful. Mohammed called them to Islam and asked them to help him in his struggles with the Meccans.

I280 Since they could not agree, Mohammed asked them to keep their meeting private. But Taif was a small town and within days everyone knew of Mohammed's presence. Mohammed kept condemning them and their kind, until one day a mob gathered and drove him out of town, pelting him with stones.

I281 Half way back to Mecca, he spent the night. When he arose for his night prayer, the Koran says that jinns came to hear him pray.

> *46:29 We sent a company of jinn so that they might hear the Koran. When the reading was finished, they returned to their people with warnings. They said, "Oh, people! We have heard a scripture sent down since the days of Moses verifying previous scriptures, a guide to the truth and the straight path. Oh, people! Hear the Messenger of Allah and believe Him that He will forgive your faults and protect you from tormenting punishment."*
>
> *46:32 Those who do not respond to Allah's messenger cannot defeat His plan on earth, and he will have no protectors beside Him. Such men are in flagrant error. Have they not seen that Allah, who created the heavens and the earth and was not wearied by their creation, can give life to the dead? Yes, He has power over all things.*
>
> *46:34 On the day the Kafirs are set before the Fire and are asked, "Is this not the truth?" They will say, "Yes, by Our Lord!" He will say, "Then taste the punishment because you did not believe." Then be patient, as the messengers had patience and firmness, and do not try to hasten their doom. When they see what has been promised them, it will be as if they had waited but one hour. Will any perish except those who have transgressed?*

PREACHING BACK IN MECCA

I282 When the Arab pilgrims came to Mecca, as they had for cen-
turies, Mohammed went out to the crowd of visitors and told them he
was the prophet of Allah and brought them the Koran.

> 11:111 *And truly your Lord will repay everyone according to their deeds for
> He is well aware of what they do.*
> 11:112 *Continue on the right path as you have been commanded—you and
> those who have turned to Allah with you—and do no wrong. He knows
> what you do. Do not depend on the evildoers for fear that the Fire will
> seize you. You have no protector beside Allah, and you will not be helped
> against Him. Observe prayer at early morning, at the close of the day, and
> at the approach of night, for good deeds drive away evil deeds. This is a
> warning for the mindful. Be patient, for Allah will not let the reward of the
> righteous perish.*
> 11:116 *Why were there not men with virtue, who were not corrupt, in the
> generations before you except the few whom we saved from harm? The
> evildoers enjoyed the selfish pleasures of earthly life, and became sinners.
> Your Lord would not destroy cities unjustly while its people were doing
> right.*
> 11:118 *If the Lord pleased, He could have made mankind of one nation, but
> only those to whom your Lord has granted His mercy will cease to differ.
> For this He created them, for the word of your Lord will be fulfilled: "I will
> completely fill Hell with jinn and men together."*

Mohammed spoke of the greatness of Allah to the Meccans and the
pilgrims.

> 42:1 *HA. MIM. AIN. SIN. KAF. Allah sends inspiration to you as He did to
> those before you. He is mighty and wise. All that is in the heavens and all
> that is in the earth is His. He is the High, the Great.*
> 42:5 *The heavens are almost split apart while the angels celebrate praise of
> their Lord and ask forgiveness for those on earth. Allah is indulgent and
> merciful. But those who take protectors besides Him—Allah watches them,
> but you have no charge over them.*
> 42:7 *So We have revealed to you an Arabic Koran so that you may warn
> the mother-city [Mecca] and all around it, and warn them of that day of
> the gathering, of which there is no doubt, when some will be in Paradise
> and some in the Flame.*
> 42:8 *If Allah had desired, He could have made them one people and of one
> creed, but He brings whom He will into His mercy. As for the evildoers,
> they will have no friend or helper. Have they taken other patrons than
> Him? Allah is the protecting friend. He gives life to the dead, and He is
> mighty over all things.*

42:10 *Whatever your differences may be, the decision rests with Allah. This is Allah, my Lord. I trust in Him and turn to Him. He is the Creator of the heavens and of the earth, and He gave you mates from among yourselves and mates for cattle, too. This is how He multiplies you. There is nothing else like Him. He is the hearer and the seer. He holds the keys of the heavens and of the earth. He gives open-handedly or He gives sparingly to whomever He desires. He knows all things.*

THE BEGINNING OF POWER AND JIHAD IN MEDINA

Although Medina was about a ten-day journey from Mecca, since ancient times the Medinans had come to Mecca for the fairs. Medina was half Jewish and half Arabian, and there was an ongoing tension between the two groups. The Jews worked as farmers and craftsmen and were literate. They were the wealthy class, but their power was slowly waning. In times past the Arabs had raided and stolen from the Jews who retaliated by saying that one day a prophet would come and lead them to victory over the Arabs. In spite of the tensions, the Arab tribe of Khazraj were allies with them.

I286 So when the members of the Khazraj met Mohammed, they said among themselves, "This is the prophet the Jews spoke of. Let us join ranks with him before the Jews do." They became Muslims, and their tribe was rancorous and divided. They hoped that Islam could unite them, and soon every house in Medina had heard of Islam.

I289 The next year when the Medinan Muslims returned to Mecca, they took an oath to Mohammed. They returned to Medina, and soon many of Medinans submitted to Islam.

I294 At the next fair in Mecca, many of the new Muslims from Medina showed up. They gave their oath to Mohammed. After the oath, one of them asked about their now severed ties to the Jews of Medina. If they helped Mohammed with arms and they were successful would he go back to Mecca? Mohammed smiled and said, "No, blood is blood, and blood not to be paid for is blood not to be paid for." Blood revenge and its obligation were common to them. "I will war against them that war against you and be at peace with those at peace with you."

THE OPENING WORDS OF WAR

I313 Up to now the main tension in the division in the Quraysh tribe over the new religion had been resolved by words. Curses and insults had been exchanged. Mohammed condemned the Meccans on an almost daily basis. The Quraysh had mocked Mohammed and abused lower class converts.

What blood had been drawn had been in the equivalent of a brawl. Dust had been thrown, but no real violence. No one had died.

IMMIGRATION

1314 The Muslim Medinans had pledged Mohammed support in war and to help the Muslims from Mecca. The Muslims in Mecca left and went to Medina. The Muslims from both Mecca and Medina were about to be tested.

> 29:1 ELIF. LAM. MIM. *Do men think that they will be left alone when they say, "We believe," and that they will not be tested? We tested those who lived before them, so Allah will surely know who is sincere and who is false. Do the ones who work evil think that they will escape Us? Their judgment is evil.*
>
> 29:5 *Whoever hopes to meet Allah, the set time will surely come. He hears and knows. Whoever makes efforts for the faith makes them for his own good only. Allah is independent of His creatures. As for those who believe and do good works, We will blot out all evil from them, and We will reward them according to their best actions.*

THE KORAN OF MEDINA

THE JEWS

CHAPTER 5

9:63 Do they not know that whoever opposes Allah
and His Messenger will abide in the Fire of Hell, where
they will remain forever? This is the great shame.

When Mohammed came to Medina Jews comprised about half the town. There were three tribes of Jews and two tribes of Arabs. The Jews were farmers and tradesmen and lived in their own fortified quarters. In general they were better educated and more prosperous than the Arabs.

Before Mohammed arrived, there had been bad blood and killing among the tribes. The last battle had been fought by the two Arab tribes, but each of the Jewish tribes had joined the battle with their particular Arab allies.

I351 The rabbis began to ask Mohammed difficult questions. But, doubts about Allah were evil. In Mecca, Mohammed had divided the community into Islam and those of the native Arabic religions. In Mecca he adopted all the classical Jewish stories to prove his prophesy and spoke well of the Jews. But there were almost no Jews living in Mecca, and therefore, no one to differ with him.

In Medina half of the population were Jews, who let Mohammed know that they disagreed with him. So in Medina, Mohammed argued with Jews as well as the Kafir Arabs. Even though there were very few in the town who were Christian, Mohammed argued against them as well. All Kafirs were verbally attacked in Medina.

THE REAL TORAH IS IN THE KORAN

Mohammed said repeatedly that the Jews and Christians corrupted their sacred texts in order to conceal the fact that he was prophesied in their scriptures. The stories in the Koran are similar to those of the Jew's scriptures, but they make different points. In the Koran, all of the stories found in Jewish scripture indicated that Allah destroyed those cultures that did not listen to their messengers.

40

1364 But the Jews did not believe that Mohammed was a prophet. As a result, they are in error and cursed by Allah. And by denying his prophethood they conspired against him and Islam.

> 2:40 *Children of Israel! Remember the favor I have given you, and keep your covenant with Me. I will keep My covenant with you. Fear My power. Believe in what I reveal [the Koran], which confirms your Scriptures, and do not be the first to disbelieve it. Do not part with My revelations for a petty price. Fear Me alone. Do not mix up the truth with lies or knowingly hide the truth [the Jews hid their scriptures that foretold Mohammed would be the final prophet]. Be committed to your prayers, give to charity regularly, and bow down with those who bow down. Would you instruct others to be righteous and forget to attend to your own duties? You read the Scriptures! Do you not have sense? Seek guidance with patience and prayer; this is indeed a hard duty, but not for the humble who remember that they will have to meet their Lord and will return to Him.*

1367 The Koran repeats the many favors that Allah has done for the Jews—they were the chosen people, delivered from slavery under the pharaoh, given the sacred Torah and all they have ever done is to sin. They have been forgiven many times by Allah, and still, they are as hard as rocks and refuse to believe Mohammed. They have perverted the Torah after understanding it.

> 2:75 *Can you believers then hope that the Jews will believe you even though they heard the Word of Allah and purposefully altered it [the Jews hid their scriptures that foretold Mohammed would be the final prophet] after they understood its meaning? And when they are among the believers they say, "We believe too," but when they are alone with one another they say, "Will you tell them what Allah has revealed to you so that they can argue with you about it in the presence of your Lord?" Do you not have any sense? Do they not realize that Allah knows what they hide as well as what they reveal?*

1369 The Jews' sins are so great that Allah has changed them into apes.

> 2:63 *And remember, Children of Israel, when We made a covenant with you and raised Mount Sinai before you saying, "Hold tightly to what We have revealed to you and keep it in mind so that you may guard against evil." But then you turned away, and if it had not been for Allah's grace and mercy, you surely would have been among the lost. And you know those among you who sinned on the Sabbath. We said to them, "You will be transformed into despised apes." So we used them as a warning to their people and to the following generations, as well as a lesson for the Allah-fearing.*

1370 The Jews have understood the truth of Mohammed and then changed their scriptures to avoid admitting that Mohammed is right.

> 5:59 *Say: Oh, people of the Book [Jews and Christians], do you not reject us only because we believe in Allah, in what He has sent down to us, in what He has sent before us, and because most of you are wrongdoers? Say: Can I tell you of retribution worse than this that awaits them with Allah? It is for those who incurred the curse of Allah and His anger; those whom He changed into apes [Jews] and swine [Christians]; those who worship evil are in a worse place, and have gone far astray from the right path.*

> 5:61 *When they presented themselves to you, they said, "We believe," but they came as Kafirs to you, and as Kafirs they left. Allah well knew what they concealed. You will see many of them striving with one another to hurry sin, to exceed limits, and to eat unlawful things. What they do is evil. Why do their doctors and rabbis not forbid them from the habit of uttering wickedness and eating unlawful food? Certainly, their works are evil.*

> 2:174 *Those [the Jews] who conceal any part of the Scriptures which Allah has revealed in order to gain a small profit shall ingest nothing but Fire in their stomachs. Allah will not speak to them on the Day of Resurrection, and they will pay a painful penalty. They are the ones who buy error at the price of guidance and torture at the price of forgiveness; how intently they seek the Fire!*

AN OMINOUS CHANGE

1381 In Mecca Mohammed spoke well of the Jews, who were very few. In Medina there were many Jews and his relations were tense. Up to now Mohammed had lead prayer in the direction of Jerusalem. Now the kiblah, direction of prayer, was changed to the Kabah in Mecca. Some of the Jews came to him and asked why he had changed the direction of prayer. After all, he said that he followed the religion of Abraham. The Koran responded:

> 2:142 *The foolish ones will say, "What makes them turn from the kiblah [the direction they faced during Islamic prayer]?" Say: Both the east and the west belong to Allah. He will guide whom He likes to the right path. We have made you [Muslims] the best of nations so that you can be witnesses over the world and so that the messenger may be a witness for you. We appointed the former kiblah towards Jerusalem and now Mecca so that We could identify the messenger's true followers and those who would turn their backs on him. It was truly a hard test, but not for those whom Allah guided. It was not Allah's purpose that your faith should be in vain, for Allah is full of pity and merciful toward mankind. We have seen you*

[Mohammed] turn your face to every part of Heaven for guidance, and now We will have you turn to a kiblah that pleases you. So turn your face towards the direction of the sacred Mosque, and wherever the believers are, they will turn their faces toward it. The People of the Book know that this is the truth from their Lord, and Allah is not unaware of what they do. Even if you were to give the People of the Book [Jews] every sign, they would not accept your kiblah, nor would you accept theirs. None of them will accept the kiblah of the others. If you should follow their way after receiving the knowledge you possess, then you will certainly be a part of the unrighteous.

62:5 Those to whom the Torah [the first five books of the Old Testament] was given and do not follow it can be compared to a donkey who is made to carry a load of books but is unable to understand them. Those who reject Allah's revelations are a sorry example. Allah does not guide those who do wrong.

4:44 Have you not thought about those [Jews] to whom a part of the Scripture was given? They buy error for themselves and wish to see you go astray from the right path. But Allah knows your enemies best. Allah is sufficient as your protector, and Allah is sufficient as your helper. Some among the Jews take words out of the context of the Scriptures and say, "We have heard, and we disobey. We hear as one who does not hear. Look at us!" in this way twisting the phrase and defiling the faith. But if they said, "We hear and obey. Hear us and look at us!" it would be better for them and more righteous. But Allah has cursed them for their disbelief; only a few of them have faith!

4:47 To those of you [Jews and Christians] to whom the Scriptures were given: Believe in what We have sent down confirming the Scriptures you already possess before We destroy your faces and twist your heads around backwards, or curse you as We did those [the Jews] who broke the Sabbath for Allah's commandments will be carried out.

THE CHRISTIANS

CHAPTER 6

33:21 You have an excellent example in Allah's Messenger
for those of you who put your hope in Allah and the
Last Day and who praise Allah continually.

I404 The few Christians in Medina argued religion with Mohammed. They held forth with the doctrine of the Trinity and the divinity of Christ. Mohammed later laid out the Islamic doctrine of the Christian doctrine. The Koran tells in detail the real story of Jesus, who is only another of Allah's prophets, and that the Trinity of the Christians is Allah, Jesus and Mary.

I406 No one has power except through Allah. Allah gave the prophet Jesus the power of raising the dead, healing the sick, making birds of clay and having them fly away. Allah gave Jesus these signs as a mark of his being a prophet. But Allah did not give the powers of appointing kings, the ability to change night to day. These lacks of power show that Jesus was a man, not part of a Trinity. If he were part of God, then all powers would have been in his command. Then he would not have to have been under the dominion of kings.

I407-8 Christ spoke in the cradle and then spoke to men as a grown man. Speaking from the cradle is a sign of his being a prophet. Christ's prophethood was confirmed by making clay birds fly. By Allah Christ healed the blind, the lepers, and raised the dead.

> *5:109 One day Allah will assemble the messengers and say, "What response did you receive from mankind?" They will say, "We have no knowledge. You are the knower of secrets." Then Allah will say, "Oh Jesus, Son of Mary, remember my favor to you and your mother when I strengthened you with the Holy Spirit [Gabriel] so that you would speak to men alike in childhood and when grown. I taught you the Scripture, wisdom, the Torah, and the Gospel, and you created the figure of a bird with clay, by my permission, and breathed into it. With My permission it became a bird. You also healed the blind and the leper, with My permission. With My permission you raised the dead. I restrained the Children of Israel from harming you when you went to them with clear signs, and the Kafirs said, "This is nothing but plain sorcery."*

5:111 *When I revealed to the disciples, "Believe in Me and the One I sent," they said, "We believe and bear witness to You that we are Muslims."*

1408 Christ only comes through Allah. Christ's signs of being a prophet come only from Allah. Jesus enjoins others to worship Allah, not him. But people refused to hear him, the Disciples came forth to help him with his mission. The Disciples were servants of Allah and were Muslims just like Christ.

1409 Christ was not crucified. When the Jews plotted against Christ, they found Allah to be the best plotter. Allah took Jesus up directly to him and will refute those who say he was crucified and was resurrected. On the final day, the Day of Resurrection, those who follow Christ but do not believe in his divinity will be blessed. Those who insist that Christ is God, part of the Trinity, and reject true faith will be punished in Hell.

3:54 *So the Jews plotted and Allah plotted, but Allah is the best of plotters. And Allah said, "Jesus! I am going to end your life on earth and lift you up to Me. [Jesus did not die on the cross. He was taken to Allah. He will return to kill the anti-Christ and then die a natural death.] I will send the Kafirs away from you and lift up those who believe above all others until the Day of Resurrection. Then all will return to Me and I will judge their disputes. As for the Kafirs, they will be punished with excruciating agony in this world and the world to come. They will have no one to help them. As for the believers who do good works, He will fully reward them. Allah does not love those who do wrong. These signs and this wise warning We bring to you."*

Although the Koran says less about Christians than Jews, it does address them.

4:171 *People of the Book [Christians]! Do not overstep the boundaries of your religion and speak only what is true about Allah. The Messiah, Jesus, the son of Mary, is only Allah's messenger and his Word which he sent into Mary was a spirit from Him. Therefore, believe in Allah and His messengers and do not say, "Trinity." Hold back and it will be better for you. Allah is only one god. Far be it from Allah to have a son! All in the heavens and earth are His. Allah is the sufficient as a protector. The Messiah does not condescend to be Allah's servant, nor do His favored angels. Those who disdain service to Him, and are filled with arrogance, Allah will gather them all together before Him.*

61:6 *And remember when Jesus, son of Mary, said, "Children of Israel! I am Allah's messenger sent to confirm the Law which was already revealed to you and to bring good news of a messenger who will come after me whose name will be Ahmad." [Ahmad was one of Mohammed's names. This quote of Jesus is not found in any Christian scriptures.] Yet when he [Moham-med] came to them with clear signs, they said, "This is merely sorcery!" And who is more evil than the one who, when called to submit to Islam, makes up a lie about Allah? Allah does not guide the evil-doers! They wish to put out Allah's light with their mouths, but as much as the Kafirs hate it, Allah will perfect His light.*

5:112 Remember when the disciples said, "Oh Jesus, Son of Mary, is your Lord able to send down a table to us spread with food from heaven?" He said, "Fear Allah if you are believers." They said, "We desire to eat from it, to satisfy hearts, to know that you have spoken the truth to us, and to be witnesses to the miracle." Jesus, Son of Mary, said, "Oh Allah, our Lord, send down a table spread with food from heaven that it will become a recurring festival from the first of us and to the last of us, and a sign from You, and do nourish us, for You are the best provider." Allah said, "I will send it down to you, but whoever among you disbelieves after that, I will surely inflict a punishment on him unlike any I have inflicted on any other creature."

5:116 And when Allah says, "Oh Jesus, Son of Mary, did you say to man-kind, 'Take me and my mother as two gods, beside Allah?'" He will say, "Glory be unto You. It is not for me to say what I had no right to say. If I had said that, You would have known it. You know what is in my heart. I do not know what is in Your heart. You know all that is hidden." "I only said what You commanded me to say, 'Worship Allah, my Lord and your Lord,' and I was a witness of their actions while I was among them. When You caused me to die, You watched them, and You are witness of all things. If You punish them, they are Your servants, and if You forgive them, You are mighty and wise."

The Koran often uses the term People of the Book. At the time of Mo-hammed there were no books in Arabic. The written Arabic was used mostly for business. Since both Christianity and Judaism used religious texts this was distinctive. The term People of the Book can refer to either Jews or Christians, or both Jews and Christians.

Muslims tell Christians and Jews they are not Kafirs, but People of the Book. However, only those Christians who believe that Jesus was not the Son of God, there is no Trinity, Jesus was not crucified, did not die and was not resurrected, and that the Gospels are a lie, are true Christians. Only those Jews who think that Mohammed was the last prophet are truly Jews.

Said another way, Christians and Jews are Kafirs, just like anybody else who does not think that Mohammed is the prophet of Allah.

THE HYPOCRITES

CHAPTER 7

47:33 Believers! Obey Allah and the messenger,
and do not let your effort be in vain.

THE HYPOCRITES

1351 Before Mohammed arrived, the Arabs were content with their religion and tolerant of others. Many Arabs became Muslims due to a pressure to join Islam. But in secret they were hypocrites who allied themselves with the Jews because they thought Mohammed was deluded.

1365 The Koran gives an analogy about the hypocrites:

> 2:8 *And some of the people [the Jews] say, "We believe in Allah and the Day," although they do not really believe. They wish to deceive Allah and His believers, but they fool no one but themselves although they do not know it. Their hearts are diseased, and Allah has increased their suffering. They will suffer an excruciating doom because of their lies.*
> 2:11 *And when they are told, "Do not make evil in the earth," they say, "We are only trying to make peace." But they truly are the evil-doers even though they do not realize it. When it is said to them, "Believe as others have believed," they say, "Should we believe as the fools believe?" They are the fools, if only they knew it! And when they meet with the faithful they say, "We believe too." But when they are alone with their fellow devils [Jews and Christians] they say, "Really, we are with you. We were only mocking them." Allah will throw their mockery back on them and leave them to wander alone in their blindness.*

1355 One of the Medinans became a Muslim and later began to doubt the truth of Mohammed and said, "If this man is right, we are worse than donkeys." Allegiance to Islam comes before family, nation, or friend. When Mohammed confronted him about his remarks and doubts, he denied it. The Koran's comments:

> 9:74 *They swear by Allah that they said nothing wrong, yet they spoke blasphemy, and some Muslims became Kafirs. They planned what they could not carry out [a plan against Mohammed], and only disapproved of it because Allah and His Messenger had enriched them by His bounty [the resistance to Mohammed decreased when the money from*

the spoils of war came into the Medinan economy]. If they repent, it will be better for them, but if they fall back into their sin, Allah will afflict them with a painful doom in this world and the next. On earth, they will have neither friend nor protector.

1357 Mohammed used to say about one of the hypocrites that he had the same face as Satan. The man used to sit and listen to Mohammed and then take back to the hypocrites what he said. He said of Mohammed, "Mohammed is all ears. If anyone tells him anything, he will believe it." The Koran speaks of him and other hypocrites:

> 9:61 *There are some of them who injure the Messenger and say, "He is only a hearer." Say: He is a hearer of good for you. He believes in Allah and believes in the faithful. He is a mercy to those of you who believe, but those who injure the Messenger of Allah will suffer a painful doom. They swear to you by Allah to please you, but Allah and His Messenger are worthier, so they should please Him if they are believers.*
> 9:63 *Do they not know that whoever opposes Allah and His Messenger will abide in the Fire of Hell, where they will remain forever? This is the great shame.*

1358 One of the hypocrites excused his criticism by saying that he was only talking and jesting. No criticism was too small to be unnoticed.

> 9:65 *If you ask them, they will surely say, "We were only talking idly and jesting." Say: Do you mock Allah, His signs, and His Messenger? Make no excuse. You have rejected faith after you accepted it. If we forgive some of you, we will punish others because they are evildoers. Hypocritical men and women have an understanding with one another. They command what is evil, forbid what is just, and do not pay the poor tax. They have forgotten Allah, and He has forgotten them. The hypocrites are the rebellious wrongdoers. Allah promises the hypocritical men and women and the Kafirs the Fire of Hell, and they will abide there; it is enough for them. Allah has cursed them, and an eternal torment will be theirs.*

1365 The hypocrites change their faces depending upon who they are with. When they are with the Muslims, they believe. But when they are with the evil ones (the Jews) they say they are with the Jews. It is the Jews who order them to deny the truth and contradict Mohammed.

> 4:138 *Warn the hypocrites that torturous punishment awaits them. The hypocrites take Kafirs as friends rather than believers. Do they look for honor at their hands? Truly all honor belongs to Allah.*

JIHAD, WAR AGAINST ALL

CHAPTER 8

4:42 On that day, the Kafirs and those who disobeyed
the Messenger will wish they could sink into the earth
for they cannot hide a single thing from Allah.

The Muslims were poor and the Meccans were rich. Then there was the matter of being driven out of Mecca and Mohammed wanted revenge. He had a idea that took care of both wealth and revenge. He would attack the Meccan caravans.

JIHAD—THE FIRST KILLING

I416-423 Mohammed sent forth his fighters on seven armed raids to find the trade caravans headed to Mecca. Not a mission found a caravan.

I423-4 Then Mohammed sent Abdullah out with eight men. They used a deception of being religious pilgrims to be able to attack, then kill and capture men and the caravan goods. The Meccans accused Mohammed of being a war criminal who had violated Arabic war code by attacking in the sacred month.

But the Koran said:

> *2:216 You are commanded to fight although you dislike it. You may hate*
> *something that is good for you, and love something that is bad for you.*
> *Allah knows and you do not. When they ask you about fighting in the holy*
> *month, say: Fighting at this time is a serious offense, but it is worse in Al-*
> *lah's eyes to deny others the path to Him, to disbelieve in Him, and to drive*
> *His worshipers out of the Sacred Mosque. Idolatry is a greater sin than*
> *murder. They will not stop fighting you until you turn away from your*
> *religion. But any of you who renounce your faith and die a Kafir, will have*
> *your works count for nothing in this world and the world to come. These*
> *people will be prisoners of the Fire, where they will live forever.*

FIGHTING IN ALLAH'S CAUSE—BADR

I428 Mohammed's luck was supreme. His enemy, Abu Sufyan, a wealthy merchant had a caravan that passed near Medina. He was able to get a small army to come from Mecca when he found Mohammed was going to attack. The ensuing battle changed the history of the world as Mohammed went to war outnumbered 3 to 1. Islam won the day.

1476 After the battle of Badr there came about an entire sura of the Koran. The Muslims were not alone. Allah sent a thousand angels to help kill the Kafirs.

> 8:2 *The true believers are the ones whose hearts tremble with fear at the mention of Allah and whose faith grows stronger when His revelations are revealed to them and in Him they put their trust. True believers are dedicated to their prayers and give generously from that which We have given them. These are truly the believers. They will be raised up and receive forgiveness from their Lord, and they will receive generous provisions.*
>
> 8:5 *Remember how your Lord commanded you to leave your homes to fight for the truth, but some of the believers were opposed to it? They disputed the truth after you had revealed it, as if they were being led to certain death before their eyes.*
>
> 8:7 *And when Allah promised that you would defeat one of the two groups of enemies, you wished to attack the group that was defenseless. [Mohammed had started out to attack a large, unarmed Meccan caravan. But a thousand-man army from Mecca arrived to protect the caravan.] But Allah wished to justify the truth of His words and to cut the Kafirs down so that the truth would triumph and the lies would be shown false, much to the opposition of the guilty.*
>
> 8:9 *Remember when you begged your Lord for help and He said, "I will send the ranks of a thousand angels to your aid?" Allah gave this as a message of good news to bring them hope for victory only comes from Allah. Allah is mighty and wise.*
>
> 8:11 *Remember when sleep overcame you, a sign of His reassurance? He sent down rain from the heavens to make you clean and to rid you of the grime of Satan, to strengthen your hearts and steady your feet. [The rain before the battle muddied the ground and hindered the Meccan cavalry.]*
>
> 8:12 *Then your Lord spoke to His angels and said, "I will be with you. Give strength to the believers. I will send terror into the Kafirs' hearts, cut off their heads and even the tips of their fingers!" This was because they opposed Allah and His messenger. Ones who oppose Allah and His messenger will be severely punished by Allah. We said, "This is for you! Taste it and know that the Kafirs will receive the torment of the Fire."*
>
> 8:15 *Believers! When you meet the Kafirs marching into battle, do not turn your back to them to retreat. Anyone who turns his back on them, unless it is for a tactical advantage or to join another company, will incur Allah's wrath and Hell will be his home, truly a tortuous end. It was not you, but Allah, that killed them. It was not you whose blows destroyed them, but*

Allah destroyed them so that He might give the believers a gift from Himself. Allah is all-hearing and all-knowing. Therefore, Allah will certainly thwart the plans of the Kafirs.

8:19 Meccans! If you sought a judgment, it has now come to you. If you cease in your persecution of the believers, it will be better for you, but if you continue in your war against the faithful, so will We continue to help them. Your vast forces will be no match for Us for Allah stands with the faithful.

1481 After war and victory there is the spoils of war. One fifth is to go to the Apostle, Allah's prophet.

8:41 Know that a fifth of all your spoils of war [the traditional cut for the leader was a fourth] belong to Allah, to His messenger, to the messenger's family, the orphans, and needy travelers. Sincerely believe in Allah and in what was sent down to you through His messenger on the day of victory when the two armies met. Allah is powerful over all things.

1482 In war (jihad) remember Allah all the time and you will prevail. Obey Mohammed, don't argue with him or each other. Don't quit, don't lose morale. Allah will see that you prevail. And when the Kafirs are slain, their troubles have just begun. Allah will use his angels to torture them forever.

8:45 Believers! When you confront their army stand fast and pray to Allah without ceasing so that you will be victorious. Obey Allah and His messenger, and do not argue with one another for fear that you will lose courage and strength. Be patient for Allah is with the patient. Do not be like the Meccans who left home bragging and full of vainglory. They prevent others from following Allah's path, but Allah knows all that they do.

8:48 Satan made their sinful acts seem acceptable to them, and he said, "No one will defeat you this day, and I will be there to help you." When the two armies came within sight of one another, however, he quickly fled saying, "I am finished with you for I can see things which you cannot [the angels were helping to kill the Kafirs]. I fear Allah for Allah's punishment is severe."

8:49 The hypocrites [Muslims who were weak in their faith] and those with diseased hearts said, "Their religion has misled the Muslims." But those who have faith in Allah will discover that Allah is mighty and wise. If only you could witness the angels carrying off the Kafirs' souls! They slash their faces and backs saying, "Taste the torment of the Fire!"

8:67 A prophet should not take prisoners of war until he has fought and slaughtered in the land. You desire the bounty of the world, but Allah desires the bounty for you of the world to come. Allah is mighty and wise. If there had not been a prior command from Allah, you would have been punished severely for what you had taken. But now enjoy the spoils you have taken, which are lawful and good, but fear Allah. Allah is forgiving and merciful.

1484 Mohammed left Mecca as a preacher and prophet. He entered Medina with about 150 Muslim converts. After a year in Medina there were about 250-300 Muslims and most of them were very poor. After the battle of Badr, a new Islam emerged. Mohammed rode out of Medina as a politician and general. Islam became an armed political force with a religious motivation, jihad.

The Koran uses the term "fighting in Allah's cause" for jihad.

2:190 And fight for Allah's cause [jihad] against those who fight you, but do not be the first to attack. Allah does not love the aggressors.

2:191 Kill them wherever you find them, and drive them out of whatever place from which they have driven you out for persecution [the Meccans made Mohammed leave] is worse than murder. But do not fight them inside the Holy Mosque unless they attack you there; if they do, then kill them. That is the reward for the Kafirs, but if they give up their ways, Allah is forgiving and merciful.

2:193 Fight them until you are no longer persecuted and the religion of Allah reigns absolute, but if they give up, then only fight the evil-doers. The defilement of a sacred month and sacred things are subject to the laws of retaliation. If anyone attacks you, attack him in the same way. Fear Allah and know that He is with those who believe.

2:195 Spend your wealth generously for Allah's cause [jihad] and do not use your own hands to contribute to your destruction. Do good, for surely Allah loves those that do good.

JIHAD, THE JEWS' EXILE

CHAPTER 9

61:11 *Believe in Allah and His messenger and fight valiantly
for Allah's cause [jihad] with both your wealth and your
lives. It would be better for you, if you only knew it!*

THE AFFAIR OF THE JEWS OF QAYNUQA

I545 There were three tribes of Jews in Medina. The Beni Qaynuqa
were gold smiths and lived in a stronghold in their quarters. It is said by
Mohammed that they broke the treaty that had been signed when Mohammed came to Medina. How they did this is unclear.

I545 Mohammed assembled the Jews in their market and said: "Oh
Jews, be careful that Allah does not bring vengeance upon you like what
happened to the Quraysh. Become Muslims. You know that I am the
prophet that was sent you. You will find that in your scriptures."

I545 They replied: "Oh Mohammed you seem to think that we are your
people. Don't fool yourself. You may have killed and beaten a few mer-
chants of the Quraysh, but we are men of war and real men."

I545 The response of the Koran:

> 3:12 *Say to the Kafirs, "Soon you will be defeated and thrown into Hell,
> a wretched home!" Truly, there has been a sign for you in the two armies
> which met in battle [at the battle of Badr, 300 Muslim defeated 1000 Mec-
> cans]. One army fought for Allah's cause, and the other army was a group
> of Kafirs, and the Kafirs saw with their own eyes that their enemy was
> twice its actual size. Allah gives help to whom He pleases. Certainly there
> is a lesson to be learned in this for those who recognize it.*

I546 Some time later Mohammed besieged the Jews in the their quarters. None of the other two Jewish tribes came to their support. Finally the
Jews surrendered and expected to be slaughtered after their capture.

I546 But an Arab ally bound to them by a client relationship ap-
proached Mohammed and said, "Oh Mohammed deal kindly with my
clients." Mohammed ignored him. The ally repeated the request and again
Mohammed ignored him. The ally grabbed Mohammed by the robe and
enraged Mohammed who said, "Let me go!" The ally said, "No, you must

deal kindly with my clients. They have protected me and now you would kill them all? I fear these changes." The response by the Koran:

> 5:51 *Oh, believers, do not take the Jews or Christians as friends. They are but one another's friends. If any one of you take them for his friends, he surely is one of them. Allah will not guide the evildoers.*
>
> 5:52 *You will see those who have a diseased heart race towards them and say, "We fear in case a change of fortune befalls us." Perhaps Allah will bring about some victory or event of His own order. Then they will repent of the thoughts they secretly held in their hearts.*
>
> 5:53 *Then the faithful will say, "Are these the men who swore their most solemn oath by Allah that they were surely with you?" Their deeds will be in vain, and they will come to ruin. Oh, you who believe, if any of you desert His religion, Allah will then raise up a people whom He will love and who will be loved by Him. They will be humble towards the faithful and haughty towards the Kafirs. They will strive hard for Allah's cause [jihad], and not fear the blame of any blamer. This is the grace of Allah. He gives to whom He pleases. Allah is all-embracing and all-knowing.*

Mohammed exiled the Jews and took all of their wealth and goods.

THE RAID TO AL QARADA

I547 Mohammed's victory at Badr and ongoing jihad caused the Quraysh to go a different route to Syria. The Muslims surprised them and the Quraysh managed to escape but Mohammed's men were able to steal all the caravan's goods, including the silver. The stolen goods were delivered to Mohammed in Medina.

KILL ANY JEW THAT FALLS INTO YOUR POWER

I554 The Apostle of Allah said, "Kill any Jew who falls into your power." Hearing this Muhayyisa fell upon a Jewish merchant who was a business associate and killed him. His brother was not a Muslim and asked him how he could kill a man who had been his friend and partner in many business deals. The Muslim said that if Mohammed had asked him to kill his brother he would have done it immediately. His brother said, "You mean that if Mohammed said to cut off my head you would do it?" "Yes," was the reply. The older brother then said, "By Allah, any religion which brings you to this is marvelous." And he decided then and there to become a Muslim.

JIHAD, A SETBACK

CHAPTER 10

> 4:14 *But those who disobey Allah and His Messenger and go beyond His limits, will be led into the Fire to live forever, and it will be a humiliating torment!*

THE BATTLE OF UHUD

I555 Back at Mecca those who had lost at the battle of Badr told others, "Men of Quraysh, Mohammed has killed your best men. Give us money so that we may take revenge." Money was raised, men were hired. An army was put together.

I558 So the Meccans camped near Medina, ready for war. Mohammed marched out with a 1000 men to meet the Meccans at the foot of Mount Uhud.

The battle went against Mohammed, because the Muslim archers disobeyed his commands and ran to get the Meccan's goods when Meccans retreated. The Meccans regrouped and won the day.

THE KORAN AND THE BATTLE OF UHUD

Since Allah had sent angels to the previous battle of Badr and the outnumbered Muslims triumphed, how could they fail at Uhud?

I593 Two of the clans of Muslims had doubts about the battle. But Allah was their friend and they did not doubt Islam and went on into the battle because of their belief in Allah and Mohammed.

> 3:121 *Remember when you [Mohammed] left your home early in the morning to lead the believers to their battle stations [battle of Uhud]? Allah heard and knew all. When two of your brigades showed cowardice, Allah protected them both. Let the faithful put their trust in Allah. Allah made you victorious at Badr when you were the weaker army. Therefore, fear Allah and be grateful to Him. Then you said to the believers, "Is it not enough for you that your Lord helped you by sending down three thousand angels?" Yes! And if you stand firm and fear Allah and you are suddenly attacked by your enemies, Allah will send down five thousand angels to wreak havoc upon them.*

3:126 *Allah intended this to be good news for you so your hearts will know peace. Victory comes from Allah alone, He is mighty and wise so that He might destroy a portion of the Kafirs, humiliate them, and keep them from their purpose. It is none of your concern whether He forgives them or punishes them for, truly, they are evil-doers. All that is in the heaven and earth belongs to Allah. He will forgive whom He pleases and punish whom He pleases. Allah is forgiving and merciful.*

I595 The reason for the loss was that the archers did not hold their ground, When they saw that the Meccans were cut off from their camp, they ran to get the spoils of war. Greed caused them to disobey Mohammed. So they should always obey Mohammed, he speaks for the Lord of all. Those who did not follow orders should ask for forgiveness. If they will see that it was their fault and be remorseful they can still get their reward of heaven.

I597 The reason that Allah let the Meccans win was to test the Muslims. Now they will know their true selves. Are they fair weather friends of Mohammed or can they see their faults? If they obey Mohammed, then they can become true Muslims. A true Muslim never loses his morale, never falls into despair.

I596 If you have been wounded or suffered losses in the battle, don't forget that the Kafirs have also suffered.

3:140 *If you have been wounded [Muslims lost the battle of Uhud], be certain that the same has already befallen your enemies. We bring misfortune to mankind in turns so that Allah can discern who are the true believers, and so that We may select martyrs from among you. Allah does not love those who do evil. It is also Allah's purpose to test the believers and to destroy the Kafirs.*

I596 The Muslims must realize that Allah will purify them through tests such as the one they have just had. Those of true faith will not be discouraged.

3:142 *Did you think that you would be permitted into Paradise before Allah tested you to see who would fight for His cause [jihad] and endure until the end? You used to wish for death before you saw it, but now that you have seen it with your own eyes, you turn and run from it. Mohammed is only a messenger, and many messengers have come before him. If he died or was killed, would you turn your backs on the faith? But those who do in fact turn their backs will not hurt Allah in the least. And Allah will surely reward those who serve Him with gratitude.*
3:145 *No soul will ever die unless it is Allah's will. The length of each life is predetermined according to the Scriptures. Those who wish to receive their*

reward in this world will receive it, and those who wish to receive their reward in the world to come will also receive it. And We will undoubtedly reward those who serve Us with gratitude.

I599 Do not think that the jihad is over. Soon Islam will bring terror to the Kafirs.

> 3:149 *Believers! If you follow the Kafirs, they will cause you to reject the faith and lead you to eternal damnation. But Allah is your protector and the best of helpers. We will strike terror into the hearts of the Kafirs because they worship others besides Allah, which He gave them no permission to do. Their home will be the Fire, a terrible resting place for the evil-doers.*

I599 Your slaughter of the Kafirs went well and you were about to wipe the Kafirs off the face of the earth, thanks to Allah. But then you disobeyed Mohammed.

> 3:152 *Allah fulfilled His covenant with you [Mohammed] when He allowed you to destroy your enemies [at the battle of Badr]. And then later, when you [the Muslims at Uhud] lost your courage, arguments broke out among you [the Muslims disobeyed orders and broke ranks to run and get the exposed spoils of the Meccans] and you sinned after you had come so close to what you wanted [spoils of war]. Some of you wish for the desires of this world and some of you for the world to come. Therefore, He caused you to be defeated so that you might be tested. Now He has forgiven you for Allah shows grace to the believers.*
> 3:153 *Remember when you [at Uhud the Muslims broke and fled] ran up the hill in cowardice and paid no attention to anyone and the messenger was behind you calling you back to the battle? Allah rewarded you with trouble for the trouble you caused Him so that you would not grieve for the spoils you lost or for what happened to you. Allah knows all that you do.*

I601 After the battle some were at ease, but others were in a state of anxiety because they did not trust Allah. The hypocrites divorced themselves from the decision and blamed others for failure. If they had their way then everyone would have been safe.

> 3:154 *Then, after the trouble Allah sent down upon you, He sent down calmness to wash over some of you. Some were overtaken by sleep, and others lay awake, stirred by their own passions, ignorantly thinking unjust thoughts about Allah. And they ask, "What do we gain by this affair?" Say: Truly the affair is entirely in Allah's hands. They hide in their hearts that which they do not want to tell you. They speak out saying, "If we had any say in this affair then none of us would have been killed here." Say: If you*

had stayed at home, those of you who were destined to be killed would have died regardless. This has taken place so that Allah might test your faith and see what is in your hearts. Allah knows the deepest secrets of every heart. Those of you who fled in cowardice on the day the two armies met in battle must have been tricked by Satan because of some evil you have done. But now Allah has forgiven you for Allah is forgiving and gracious.

Those who die in jihad will be rewarded by Allah.

3:156 Believers! Do not follow the Kafirs' example when they say about their brothers who have been killed in a foreign country or in battle, "If only they had stayed at home they would not have died or have been killed!" Allah will make them regret what they have said. Allah is the giver of both life and death; Allah knows all that you do.
3:157 The forgiveness and mercy they, who die or are killed for Allah's cause, will receive from Allah will be far better than anything they could have gained. If you die or are killed, then surely you will all be gathered before Allah.

I603 The Muslim's loss was a test that was brought on by their decisions.

3:165 And when disaster [battle of Uhud] befell you, although it brought destruction twice as great to the Kafirs, you said, "Why is this happening to us?" Say to them, "You have brought this upon yourselves for Allah controls all things. The destruction which befell you the day the two armies met in battle was Allah's will so He would recognize who were the true believers and who were the hypocrites." And when they were told, "Come and fight for Allah's cause [jihad] and drive your enemies back," they replied, "If we knew how to fight, then we would have followed you."
3:168 Some of them were closer to unbelief than faith that day. What they said with their mouths was not what was in their hearts, but Allah knew what they were hiding in their hearts. It was these who said, while sitting at home, of their brothers, "If only they had listened to us, then they would not have been killed." Say: Try to avert your death if what you say is true!
3:169 Never believe that those who have been killed for Allah's cause [jihad] are dead. No, they are alive with their Lord and receive rich provisions. They rejoice in the bounty Allah gives them and are joyful for those left behind who have yet to join them that they will have nothing fear or regret. They are filled with joy for Allah's grace and blessings. Allah will not fail to reward the faithful.
3:172 As for those who answered the call of Allah and His messenger after they were defeated [battle of Uhud], those of them who do good works and fear Allah will be richly rewarded. They are the ones who when it was said to them, "Your enemies are gathering vast armies against you, so fear them," it only increased their faith and they said, "Allah's help is enough

for us. He is the most excellent protector." It was in this manner that they earned Allah's grace and blessings, and no harm came to them. And they worked to please Allah for Allah is full of boundless grace.

1606 The success that the Kafirs are experiencing is temporary. They will grow in their evil and they will be punished. Allah will not leave the believers in this state. But this trial will separate the weak from the strong. Those who have wealth should spend it on Allah's cause.

> 3:175 *It is only Satan who causes you to fear his followers [the leaders of the Meccans]. Do not fear them; fear Me if you are truly believers. Do not be distressed for those who turn away from the faith for Allah is not hurt by them. Allah will refuse them any part of the world to come. Severe torment awaits them. Those who trade their faith for unbelief will do no harm to Allah, and they will receive a painful punishment.*
>
> 3:178 *Do not let the Kafirs think that we lengthen their days for their own good. We give them time only hoping that they will commit more serious sins. They will receive a shameful punishment.*

ASSASSINATION AS JIHAD

After Uhud, several Arabian tribes allied themselves under the leadership of Sufyan Ibn Khalid. Mohammed dispatched an assassin to kill him, for without his leadership the coalition would fall apart. So the assassin, killed Sufyan, cut off his head and went back to Medina.

Abdullah presented Mohammed with the head of his enemy. Mohammed was gratified and presented him with his walking stick. He said, "This is a token between you and me on the day of resurrection. Very few will have such to lean on in that day." Abdullah attached it to his sword scabbard.

JIHAD, THE JEWS SUBMIT

CHAPTER 11

> 58:20 *Those who oppose Allah and His Messenger will be laid*
> *low. Allah has declared, "Surely I will be victorious, along*
> *with My messengers." Truly Allah is strong and mighty.*

CLEANSING

I653 Mohammed attacked the second of the three Jewish tribes in Medina. He raised his army and went off to put their fortresses under siege. These Jews grew the finest dates in all of Arabia. So Mohammed cut and burned their date palms as they watched. He was accused of breaking Arabic war code.

I653 Now the other Jewish tribe had assured them that they would come to their defense. But no Jew would stand with another Jew against Islam. With no help from their brothers, the besieged Jews cut a deal with the apostle of Allah. They were relieved of their goods and were exiled.

I654 There were some new problems created—the burning of the date palms. The Koran had the answers.

> 59:2 *It was He who caused the People of the Book [the Jews] to leave their*
> *homes and go into the first exile. They did not think they would leave, and*
> *they thought that their fortresses could protect them from Allah. But Al-*
> *lah's wrath reached them from where they did not expect it and cast terror*
> *into their hearts, so that they destroyed their homes with their own hands,*
> *as well as by the hands of the believers. Take warning from this example,*
> *you who have the eyes to see it!*
> 59:3 *And if Allah had not decreed their exile, surely He would have pun-*
> *ished them in this world. And in the world to come they will receive the*
> *punishment of the Fire because they had disobeyed Allah and His Mes-*
> *senger. Whoever disobeys Allah, knows that Allah is truly severe in His*
> *punishment.*
> 59:5 *Allah gave you permission to cut down some palm trees and leave*
> *others intact so as to shame the wicked [the Jews]. After Allah gave the*
> *spoils to His Messenger, you made no move with horses or camels to cap-*
> *ture them [the Jews], but Allah gives His messengers power over what He*
> *chooses. Allah is all-powerful.*

THE BATTLE OF THE TRENCH

I669 The Meccans put together an army and set out to attack Mohammed. As Mohammed had many spies in Mecca, so it took no time until he knew of the coming fight and he built a defensive trench.

I677-683 The trench defense frustrated the Meccans. The weather was bad and the allies were distrustful of each other. In terms of actual combat only a handful of men were killed over the twenty-day siege. The Meccans broke camp and went back home. It was a victory for Mohammed.

> 33:9 *Believers! Remember Allah's grace when your enemies attacked you [the Battle of the Ditch], and We set a mighty wind against them [the Meccans and their allies, the confederates, put Medina under siege], and warriors they could not see, but Allah sees clearly all that you do. [The confederates' poor planning, poor leadership, and bad weather caused them to fail]*
>
> 33:10 *When they attacked you from above and from below, your eyes went wild, your hearts leapt up into your throats, and you doubted Allah's strength. There were the believers tried, and they were severely shaken. The hypocrites and the diseased of heart said, "Allah and His Messenger promised us only to deceive us." A group of them said, "People of Medina! It is not safe for you here. Therefore, go back to your city." Then another group said, "Our homes have been left defenseless," although they were not, and they really only wanted to run away.*
>
> 33:14 *If the enemy had infiltrated the entire city, the disaffected would have been incited to rebel, and they surely would have done so, but they would have maintained control for only a short while. Before they had pledged to Allah that they would never turn their backs and flee. A pledge to Allah must be answered for. Say: Fleeing will not help you. If you are running away from death or slaughter, even if you do escape, you will only be left to enjoy this world for a short time. Say: Who will keep you from Allah if it is His will to punish you or to show you mercy? Only Allah is your guardian and a helper.*

THE SOLUTION FOR THE JEWS

I684 After the battle Mohammed put the Jews under siege for twenty-five days. Finally, the Jews offered to submit their fate to a Muslim, Saad, with whom they had been an ally in the past. His judgment was simple. Kill all the men. Take their property and take the women and children as captives. Mohammed said, "You have given the judgment of Allah."

I690 The captives were taken into Medina. They dug trenches in the market place of Medina. It was a long day, but 800 Jews met their death that day. Mohammed and his twelve year old wife sat and watched the entire day and into the night. The Apostle of Allah had every male Jew killed.

I693 Mohammed took the property, wives and children of the Jews, and divided it up amongst the Muslims. Mohammed took his one fifth of the slaves and sent a Muslim with the female Jewish slaves to a nearby city where the women were sold for pleasure. Mohammed invested the money from the sale of the female slaves for horses and weapons.

I693 There was one last piece of spoils for Mohammed. The most beautiful Jewess was his for pleasure.

I696-7 In the battle of the Trench it was Allah who had won the day. Allah is what gives the Muslim his strength and will. No matter what the Kafirs do Allah will triumph.

> 33:25 *And Allah drove back the Kafirs in their wrath, and they gained nothing by it. Allah aided the believers in the war, for Allah is strong and mighty. He brought down some of the People of the Book [the Jews] out of their fortresses to aid the confederates and to strike terror into their hearts. Some you killed, and others you took captive. He made you heirs of their land, their homes, and their possessions, and even gave you another land on which you had never before set foot. Allah has power over everything. [800 male Jews were executed, their property taken, and women and children enslaved.]*

The Koran's last words about the Jews:

> 5:12 *Allah did, of old, make a covenant with the children of Israel, and We appointed twelve leaders among them, and Allah said, "I will be with you if you observe regular prayer, practice regular charity, believe in My messengers and help them, and offer Allah goodly gifts. I will surely wipe away your sins, and I will bring you into Gardens beneath which the rivers flow. Whoever of you does not believe this has gone astray from the even path."*
> 5:13 *Because they [the Jews] broke their covenant, We have cursed them and have hardened their hearts. They changed the words of Scripture [Islam claims that the Jews removed the references to Mohammed's coming from their Scripture] from their places and have forgotten part of what they were taught. You will always discover them in deceits, except for a few of them, but forgive them and overlook their misdeeds. Allah loves those who act generously.*

MOHAMMED'S FAMILY LIFE

CHAPTER 12

*48:13 We have prepared a blazing Fire for these Kafirs
who do not believe in Allah and His Messenger.*

Mohammed had many wives. The Koran goes into detail about his romances.

THE LIE

When Mohammed went on his missions to attack those who resisted Islam, he took Aisha with him on this trip to fight in Allah's cause in attacking the Mustaliq tribe.

I731 When the tent had been struck and the men in charge loaded the howdah on the camel and off they went without Aisha. When she got back the entire group had moved on. She returned on a camel led by a young Muslim who had lagged behind the main body and brought her back to Medina.

I732 Tongues began to wag, imaginations worked overtime and gossip spread. Tempers flared and men offered to kill the gossips. In the end the innocence or guilt of Aisha was determined by revelation in the Koran which to this day is the Sharia (Islamic law) about adultery.

> *24:1 A sura [chapter] which We have sent down and ordained, and in which We give you clear signs so that you will take warning. The man and woman who commit adultery should each be beaten with a hundred lashes, and do not let your pity for them prevent you from obeying Allah. If you believe in Allah and the Last Day, then allow some of the believers to witness their punishment. An adulterer can only marry an adulteress or an Kafir, and a adulteress cannot marry anyone other than an adulterer or an Kafir. Such marriages are forbidden for believers.*
> *24:4 Those who make accusations against honorable women and are unable to produce four witnesses should be given eighty lashes. Thereafter, do not accept their testimony, for they are terrible sinners, except those who repent afterwards and live righteously. Allah is truly forgiving and merciful.*
> *24:6 If a husband accuses his wife of adultery but he has no witnesses other than himself, his evidence can be accepted if he swears by Allah four times that he is telling the truth and then calls down Allah's curse upon him if he*

is lying. If, however, the wife swears by Allah four times that she is innocent and calls Allah's curse down upon herself if she is lying, then she should not be punished.

24:10 *If it were not for Allah's grace and mercy towards you and that Allah is wise, this would not have been revealed to you.*

24:11 *Truly there is a group among you who spread that lie [During an armed raid, Aisha—Mohammed's favorite wife since their marriage when she was age six—accidentally spent a day alone with a young jihadist. Gossip about what might have happened consumed the Muslims], but do not think of it as a bad thing for you [Aisha was cleared of doubt of sexual infidelity by a revelation in the Koran] for it has proved to be advantageous for you. Every one of them will receive the punishment they have earned. Those who spread the gossip will receive a torturous punishment.*

24:12 *Why did the believing men and women, when they heard this, not think better of their own people and say, "This is an obvious lie"? Why did they not bring four witnesses? And because they could not find any witnesses, they are surely liars in Allah's sight.*

24:14 *If it were not for Allah's goodness towards you and His mercy in this world and the world to come, you would have been severely punished for the lie you spread. You [the Muslims] gossiped about things you knew nothing about. You may have thought it to be only a light matter, but it was a most serious one in Allah's sight. And why, when you heard it, did you not say, "It is not right for us to talk about this. Oh, Allah! This is a serious sin." Allah warns you never to repeat this if you are true believers. Allah makes His signs clear to you, for Allah is all-knowing, wise. Those who take pleasure in spreading foul rumors about the faithful will be severely punished in this world and the world to come. And Allah knows, while you do not.*

Since there were not four witnesses, then there was no adultery and the gossips received eighty lashes.

33:50 *Messenger! We allow you your wives whose dowries you have paid, and the slave-girls Allah has granted you as spoils of war, and the daughters of your paternal and maternal uncles and aunts who fled with you to Medina, and any believing woman who gives herself to the Messenger, if the Messenger wishes to marry her. This is a privilege for you only, not for any other believer. We know what We have commanded the believers concerning wives and slave-girls. We give you this privilege so you will be free from blame. Allah is forgiving and merciful!*

33:51 *You may turn away any of them that you please, and take to your bed whomever you please, and you will not be blamed for desiring one you had previously set aside for a time. Therefore, it will be easier for you to comfort them and prevent their grief and to be content with what you give each of them. Allah knows what is in your hearts, and Allah is all-knowing and gracious.*

33:52 *It will be unlawful for you to marry more wives after this or to exchange them for other wives, even though you are attracted by their beauty, except slave-girls you own. [Mohammed had nine wives and several slave-girls.] And Allah watches over all things.*

MARY, THE COPTIC SLAVE OF PLEASURE

Mohammed was given two Coptic (Egyptian Christian) slaves. One he gave to another Muslim, but he kept Mary, fair of skin with curly hair. He did not move her into the harem, but set up an apartment in another part of Medina. Mary gave something in sex that none of his wives could—a male child, Ibrahim. Mohammed doted on him.

The harem was jealous. The wives banded together against Mary and it was a house of anger and coldness. Mohammed withdrew and swore he would not see his wives for a month and lived with Mary.

The Koran:

66:1 *Why, Oh, Messenger, do you forbid yourself that which Allah has made lawful to you? Do you seek to please your wives? [Mohammed was fond of a Coptic (Egyptian Christian) slave named Mary. Hafsa found Mohammed in her room with Mary, a violation of Hafsa's domain. He told a jealous Hafsa that he would stop relations with Mary and then did not. But Hafsa was supposed to be quiet about this matter.] Allah is lenient and merciful. Allah has allowed you release from your oaths, and Allah is your master. He is knowing and wise.*

66:3 *When the Messenger confided a fact to one of his wives, and when she divulged it, [Hafsa had told Aisha (Mohammed's favorite wife) about Mary and the harem became embroiled in jealousy.] Allah informed Mohammed of this, and he told her [Hafsa] part of it and withheld part. When Mohammed told her of it, she said, "Who told you this?" He said, "He who is knowing and wise told me."*

66:4 *"If you both [Hafsa and Aisha] turn in repentance to Allah, your hearts are already inclined to this, but if you conspire against the Messenger, then know that Allah is his protector, and Gabriel, and every just man among the faithful, and the angels are his helpers besides. Perhaps, if he [Mohammed] divorced you all, Allah would give him better wives than you—Muslims, believers, submissive, devout, penitent, obedient, observant of fasting, widows, and virgins."*

Ibrahim became a favorite of Mohammed. But when the child was fifteen months old, he fell sick. Mary and her slave sister attended the child during his illness. Mohammed was there at his death and wept mightily.

Mohammed was to suffer the Arabic shame of having no living male children to succeed him.

MARRIAGE TO HIS DAUGHTER-IN-LAW

Mohammed had an adopted son, Zaid, and was attracted to his wife. Zaid divorced her. In Arabia a union between a man and his daughter-in-law was incest and forbidden. But while Mohammed was with Aisha, he had a revelation and said, "Who will go and congratulate Zeinab and tell her that Allah has blessed our marriage?" The maid went right off to tell her of the good news. So Mohammed added another wife to his harem.

> 33:4 *Allah has not given any man two hearts for one body, nor has He made your wives whom you divorce to be like your mothers, nor has He made your adopted sons like your real sons. [Previous to this verse, an Arab's adopted children were treated as blood children. This verse relates to verse 37 below.] These are only words you speak with your mouths, but Allah speaks the truth and guides to the right path. Name your adopted sons after their real fathers; this is more just in Allah's sight.*

> 33:36 *And it is not the place of a believer, either man or woman, to have a choice in his or her affairs when Allah and His Messenger have decided on a matter. Those who disobey Allah and His Messenger are clearly on the wrong path. And remember when you said to your adopted son [Zaid], the one who had received Allah's favor [converted to Islam], "Keep your wife to yourself and fear Allah," and you hid in your heart what Allah was to reveal, and you feared men [what people would say if he married his daughter-in-law], when it would have been right that you should fear Allah. And when Zaid divorced his wife, We gave her to you as your wife, so it would not be a sin for believers to marry the wives of their adopted sons, after they have divorced them. And Allah's will must be carried out.*

Since Zaid was adopted, he was not really a son, so there was no incest.

It was about this time that the veil was imposed. The wives became mothers of the faithful and could not marry after Mohammed died.

> 33:55 *There is no blame on the Messenger's wives if they speak unveiled with their fathers, sons, brothers, nephews on either their brother's or sister's side, their women, or their slave-girls. Women! Fear Allah, for Allah witnesses all things.*

MOHAMMED'S FINAL JIHAD

CHAPTER 13

3:53 "Our Lord! We believe in what Thou hast
revealed, and we follow the Apostle; then write
us down among those who bear witness."

KHAYBAR

1756 After the treaty of Al Hudaybiya, Mohammed stayed in Medina for about two months before he collected his army and marched to the forts of Khaybar, a community of wealthy Jewish farmers who lived in a village of separate forts about 100 miles from Medina.

1758 Mohammed seized the forts one at a time. Among the captives was a beautiful Jewess named Safiya. Mohammed took her for his sexual pleasure. One of his men had first chosen her for his own slave of pleasure, but Mohammed traded him two of her cousins for Safiya.

1759 On the occasion of Khaybar, Mohammed put forth new orders about the sex with captive women.

1764 Mohammed knew that there was a large treasure hidden somewhere in Khaybar, so he brought forth the Jew who he thought knew the most about it and had him tortured and then beheaded.

1764 At Khaybar Mohammed instituted the first *dhimmis*. A dhimmi has no civil rights and lives under Sharia law. After the best of the goods were taken from the Jews Mohammed left them to work the land. They gave Mohammed half of their profits as the *jizya*, the dhimmi tax.

THE PILGRIMAGE

1789 After returning from Khaybar, Mohammed sent out many raiding parties and expeditions. Seven years after Mohammed moved to Medina and one year after the treaty of Hudaybiya, Mohammed led the Muslims to the Kabah in Mecca. While there he kissed one of the stones of the Kabah and trotted around the Kabah. When he got to the corner with the Black Stone, he walked up and kissed it. He did this for three circuits of the Kabah.

1790 After his three day stay in Mecca, the Quraysh asked him to leave as per the treaty. Mohammed asked to stay and have a wedding feast and he would invite the Quraysh. The Quraysh said no, please leave. He left.

THE RAID ON MUTA

1791-3 Mohammed sent an army of 3000 to Muta soon after his return from Mecca. Now Muta was north of Medina, near Syria. When they arrived the Muslims found a large army of the Byzantines. The Muslims were cut to ribbons. The Byzantines were professionals and superior in numbers.

MECCA CONQUERED

1803 At the treaty of Hudaybiya, it was agreed that the Meccans and Mohammed could make alliances between themselves and other tribes.

1811 As a result of the fighting between a tribe allied with the Meccans and a tribe allied with Mohammed, he marched on Mecca with 10,000 men to punish them.

1819 Mohammed had told his commanders only to kill those who had spoken against Mohammed. The list of those to be killed:

- One of Mohammed's secretaries, who had said that when he was recording Mohammed's Koranic revelations sometimes Mohammed let the secretary insert better speech. This caused him to lose faith and he became an apostate.
- Two singing girls who had sung satires against Mohammed.
- A Muslim tax collector who had become an apostate (left Islam).
- A man who had insulted Mohammed.

THE BATTLE OF HUNAIN

1840 When Mohammed took Mecca, the surrounding Arab tribes saw that if he was not opposed he would be King of Arabia. The Hawazin Arabs decided to oppose him under the leadership of Malik.

1842 He borrowed armor and lances from a wealthy Meccan and then marched out with 12,000 men.

1845 The Muslims almost lost the day.

> 9:25 *Allah has helped you in many battlefields, and on the day of Hunain, when your great numbers elated you [there were 12,000 Muslims and 4000 Kafirs], but availed you nothing [the Muslims panicked and fled], and the earth, for all its breadth, constrained you, you turned your backs in flight.*
> 9:26 *Then Allah sent down His tranquility on His Messenger and on the faithful, and He sent down invisible forces and He punished the Kafirs.*

This is the reward for those without faith. After this, Allah will turn to whom He pleases, for Allah is oft-forgiving and merciful.

THE RAID ON TABUK

1894 Mohammed decided to raid the Byzantines. The men began to prepare, but with no enthusiasm due to the heat, it was time for harvest to begin and they remembered the last combat with the Byzantines—they lost badly.

But the Koran had a comment:

> 9:45 *The only ones who will ask leave of you are those who do not believe in Allah and the Last Day, whose hearts are full of doubts, and who waver in their doubts. If they had intended to go to war, they would have prepared for war. But Allah was opposed to their marching forth and held them back. It was said, "Sit at home with those who sit." If they had taken the field with you, they would not have added to your strength but would have hurried about among you, stirring up dissension. Some of you would have listened to them. Allah knows the evildoers. They had plotted dissension before and made plots against you again until the truth arrived. Then the decree of Allah prevailed, much to their disgust.*

1902 When they got to Tabuk, the Christians there paid the poll tax, jizya. By paying the poll tax, a per person tax, they would not be attacked, killed or robbed by the Muslims. Those who paid the jizya were under the protection of Islam

ETERNAL JIHAD

After all the victories, some Muslims said that the days of fighting were over and even began to sell their arms. However, jihad was recognized as the normal state of affairs. Indeed, the Koran prepares the way for this:

> 9:122 *The faithful should not all go out together to fight. If a part of every troop remained behind, they could instruct themselves in their religion and warn their people when they return to them that they should guard against evil.*
> 9:123 *Believers, fight the Kafirs who are near you, and let them find you to be tough and hard. Know that Allah is with those who guard against evil.*

Sura 9, the last chapter of the Koran contains the infamous Sword Verse:

> 9:5 *When the sacred months [by ancient Arab custom there were four months during which there was to be no violence] are passed, kill the Kafirs wherever you find them. Take them as captives, besiege them, and lie in wait for them with every kind of ambush. If they submit to Islam, observe*

prayer, and pay the poor tax, then let them go their way. Allah is gracious and merciful.

1924 The Koran then turns to the issue of the raid on the Byzantines at Tabuk. Muslims must answer the call to jihad. It is an obligation. If the Byzantine raid had been short and had made for easy war spoils, the Muslims would have joined readily. But instead they made excuses. A Muslim's duty is not to avoid fighting with their person and money.

9:38 *Oh, believers, what possessed you that when it was said, "March forth in Allah's cause [jihad]," you cling heavily to the earth? Do you prefer the life of this world to the next? Little is the comfort of this life compared to the one that is to come. Unless you march forth, He will punish you with a grievous penalty, and He will put another in your place. You will not harm Him at all, for Allah has power over everything.*

9:40 *If you do not assist your Messenger, it is no matter for Allah assisted him when the Kafirs drove him out, he [Mohammed] being only one of two men. When the two [Mohammed and Abu Bakr] were in the cave, the Messenger said to his companion, "Do not be distressed, for Allah is with us." Allah sent His tranquility upon him, and strengthened him with hosts you did not see. He humbled the word of those who disbelieved and exalted the word of Allah, for Allah is mighty and wise. March forth both the lightly and heavily armed, and strive hard in Allah's cause [jihad] with your substance and your persons. This is better for you if you know it.*

1926 Those who try to avoid jihad are hypocrites. The Prophet should struggle against them. They are bound for Hell.

9:73 *Oh, Prophet, strive hard against the Kafirs and the hypocrites, and be firm with them. Hell will be their dwelling place: A wretched journey.*

A SUMMARY OF MOHAMMED'S ARMED EVENTS

1973 In a nine year period Mohammed personally attended 27 raids. There were 38 other battles and expeditions. This is a total of 65 armed events, not including assassinations and executions, for an average of one violent event every six weeks. He died without an enemy left standing.

CHRISTIANS AND JEWS

CHAPTER 14

24:51 But when Allah and His Messenger call
the true believers to judge between them, their
response is, "We have heard, and we obey."

THE FINAL STATE OF CHRISTIANS AND JEWS

When Mohammed first started preaching in Mecca, his religion was Arabian. Then Allah became identified with Jehovah and Jewish elements were introduced. When Mohammed moved to Medina, he argued with the Jews when they denied his status as a prophet in the Judaic line. He then annihilated the Jews and makes no more connections between Islam and Judaism. In his last statement, Jews and Christians became perpetual second class political citizens, dhimmis (pay the dhimmi tribute, jizya, and are subdued). Only those Christians and Jews who submit to Islam are protected. Islam defines Judaism and Christianity. The real Christians are those who deny the Trinity and accept Mohammed as the final prophet. The real Jews are those who accept Mohammed as the final prophet of their god, Jehovah. Both Christians and Jews must accept that the Koran is the true Scripture and accept that the Old Testament and New Testament are corrupt and in error. The contradictions between the Koran and the New and Old Testament are proof of the corruption of the Kafirs.

All other Jews and Christians follow false religion and are Kafirs.

> *9:29 Make war on those who have received the Scriptures [Jews and Christians] but do not believe in Allah or in the Last Day. They do not forbid what Allah and His Messenger have forbidden. The Christians and Jews do not follow the religion of truth until they submit and pay the poll tax [jizya], and they are humiliated.*

The Christians have hidden their prophesies that reveal Mohammed would come to fulfill the work of Christ. To believe in the divinity of Christ is to refuse to submit to Islam. Those Christians are Kafirs and infidels. Like the Jews, only those Christians who submit to Islam and become dhimmis who are ruled by the Sharia (Islamic law) are actual Christians. Islam defines all religions. No religion defines itself, except Islam.

5:14 *We made a covenant with those who say, "We are Christians," but they, too, have forgotten a part of what they were taught [Islam claims that the Christians suppressed the prophecies of Jesus that Mohammed would be the final prophet] so We have stirred up animosity and hatred among them that will last until Resurrection Day. In the end, Allah will tell them what they have done.*

5:15 *Oh, people of the Scriptures, Our Messenger has come to you to clear up what you have hidden of those Scriptures and to pass over many things that are now unnecessary. Now you have a new light and a clear Book from Allah. He will use it to guide whoever seeks to follow His good pleasure to paths of peace. He will bring them out of the darkness to the light, and, by his decree, will guide them to the straight path.*

5:17 *Surely they are Kafirs who say, "Allah is the Messiah, son of Mary." Say: Who has any power against Allah if He chose to destroy the Messiah, son of Mary, his mother, and all who are on the earth together? Allah's is the sovereignty of the heavens and of the earth and of all that is between them. He creates what He will, and Allah has power over all things.*

5:72 *The Kafirs say, "Jesus is the Messiah, Son of Mary," for the Messiah said, "Oh, Children of Israel, worship Allah, my Lord and your Lord." Whoever will join other gods with Allah, He will forbid him in the Garden, and his abode will be the Fire. The wicked will have no helpers. They surely blaspheme who say, "Allah is the third of three [the Trinity]," for there is no god except one Allah, and if they do not refrain from what they say, a grievous penalty will fall on those who disbelieve. Will they not turn to Allah and ask His forgiveness? For Allah is forgiving and merciful.*

5:75 *The Messiah, Son of Mary, is but a messenger. Other messengers have passed away before him, and his mother was a saintly woman; they both ate food. See how Allah makes His signs clear to them; then see how they turn from the truth. Say: Will you worship, beside Allah, that which can neither hurt nor help you? Allah hears and knows all things.*

THE SHARIA

CHAPTER 15

> 4:170 *People! The Messenger has come to you with truth*
> *from your Lord. If you believe, it will be better for you.*

The Sharia is the law of Islam that is based upon the Koran, the Hadith and the Sira. It is the political aim of Islam to replace all legal codes and constitutions (which are man-made) with the Sharia, which comes from Allah. Most of the Sharia is based on the Sunna (examples) of Mohammed. But here are some of the verses that show how the Sharia is formed.

MARRIAGE/DIVORCE/SEX

Mohammed repeated the points in this verse about women in his last speech at Mecca.

> 4:34 *Allah has made men superior to women because men spend their wealth to support them. Therefore, virtuous women are obedient, and they are to guard their unseen parts as Allah has guarded them. As for women whom you fear will rebel, admonish them first, and then send them to a separate bed, and then beat them. But if they are disobedient after that, then do nothing further; surely Allah is exalted and great!*
>
> 4:35 *If you fear a breach between a man and wife, then send a judge from his family, and a judge from her family. If they both want to come to a reconciliation, Allah will bring them back together. Truly Allah is all-knowing and wise!*

> 24:30 *Tell the men who are believers that they should look away from that which tempts them and control their lustful desires. Therefore, they will be more pure. Allah is well aware of all they do. And tell the women who are believers that they should lower their eyes and guard their purity, and they should not display their beauty and adornments except that which is normally shown. They should cover their breasts with their veils and only show their adornments to their husband, father-in-law, sons, step-sons, brothers, nephews, or their female servants, eunuch slaves, and children who are innocent and do not notice a woman's nakedness. And do not let them stamp their feet so as to reveal their hidden adornments [ankle bracelets]. Believers, all of you turn to Allah and repent so that it will go well for you.*

24:32 *And marry those among you who are single, or an honorable male or female servant. And if they are poor, then Allah will give them riches from His own bounty. Allah is bountiful and all-knowing. And for those who cannot afford to marry, let them stay pure until Allah fulfills their needs from His bounty. In regard to your slaves who wish to buy their freedom, grant it if you see there is good in them, and give them a part of the wealth that Allah has given you. Do not force your female slaves into prostitution just to gain the wealth of this world if they wish to remain pure. Yet if they are forced to do so, then truly Allah will be merciful.*

2:221 *You will not marry pagan women unless they accept the faith. A slave girl who believes is better than an idolatress, although the idolatress may please you more. Do not give your daughters away in marriage to Kafirs until they believe for a slave who is a believer is better than an idolater, though the idolater may please you more. These lure you to the Fire, but Allah calls you to Paradise and forgiveness by His will. He makes His signs clear to mankind so that they may remember.*

This next verse is the basis for sexual relations between a man and his wife.

2:223 *Your women are your plowed fields: go into your fields when you like, but do some good deed beforehand and fear Allah. Keep in mind that you will meet Him. Give good news to the believers.*

4:15 *If any of your women are guilty of adultery or fornication, then bring in four of you as witnesses against them. If they admit their guilt, then shut them up in their houses until they die or until Allah makes some other way for them. If two of your men are guilty of an indecent act [homosexuality], punish both of them. If they ask for forgiveness and change their ways, then leave them alone, for Allah is forgiving and merciful!*

4:17 *Allah will forgive those who sin unknowingly and then turn away and repent soon thereafter; Allah will show them mercy, for Allah is knowing and wise! But as for those who do evil, and then when they are about to die say, "Now I truly turn to Allah!" or those who die as Kafirs, they will not be forgiven, and a painful punishment is prepared for them.*

4:19 *Believers! It is not allowed for you to inherit the wives of your deceased family members against their will, or to prevent the wives from re-marrying in order to take away part of the dowry you have given them unless they are guilty of flagrant indecency. Treat them kindly for if you hate them, it may be that you hate that in which Allah has placed abundant goodness.*

4:20 *If you want to exchange one wife for another, do not take anything away from the dowry you have given her. Would you take it by slandering her and doing her obvious wrong? How could you take it back when you have slept with one another and entered into a firm covenant?*

LEGAL

5:38 As to the thieves, whether men or women, cut off their hands in payment for their deeds. This is a penalty by way of warning from Allah Himself. Allah is mighty and wise. But whoever repents after his wickedness, and makes amends, Allah will turn to him, for Allah is forgiving and merciful. Do you not know that the sovereignty of the heavens and of the earth is Allah's? He punishes whom He will and forgives whom He will. Allah has power over all things.

2:178 Believers! Retaliation is prescribed for you in the matter of murder: the free man for the free man, a slave for a slave, a female for a female. If the brother of the slain gives a measure of forgiveness, then grant him any sensible request, and compensate him with a generous payment [blood money]. This is a merciful indulgence from your Lord. He who sins after having been pardoned will suffer a terrible fate. And there is life for you in the law of retaliation, men of understanding, so that you will protect yourselves against evil.

2:180 It is ordered that when you are on the verge of death that you dispense your possessions equally to parents and near relatives. This is the duty of the Allah-fearing. One who hears the will and then changes it will be guilty, for Allah is all-hearing and all-knowing. But if anyone fears an error or partiality on the part of the testator and brings about an agreement among the parties, then he is not to blame. Allah is forgiving and merciful.

4:92 A believer should never kill a Muslim unless an accident occurs. Whoever kills a fellow Muslim by accident must free one of his believing slaves and pay blood-money to the victim's family unless they give it to charity. If the victim was a believer from a people at war with you, then freeing a believing slave is enough. But if the victim was from a people with whom you have an alliance, then his family should be paid blood-money and a believing slave must be set free. For those who cannot afford to do this, they must fast for two months straight. This is the penance commanded by Allah. Allah is all-knowing and wise!

4:93 For those who intentionally kill another Muslim, Hell will be their punishment, where they will live forever. The wrath of Allah will be upon them, He will curse them, and they will receive terrible torture.

COMMENTS

CHAPTER 16

THE STORY OF THE KORAN

When Mohammed's life is woven back into the Koran, the Koran is transformed. It starts with prayers and praise to the Creator and ends in a political triumph over all enemies, then and now.

The Koran of Mecca is generally religious with one theme: obey the prophets of Allah. Obey Mohammed or burn in Hell. The Koran of Medina changes the message to: obey Mohammed or suffer destruction in this life, jihad. Harming Kafirs is a political act. This is a political message.

Contradiction is at the core of the Koran, what is said at one time can be contradicted at a later time.

The Koran is highly derivative. Judgment day, Paradise, Hell, Moses, Noah and the other familiars from Christianity and Judaism stand out. Images and concepts from Zoroastrianism are used. The odd versions of Christianity and Judaism are found in vanished heretical Arab churches and Jewish commentaries. Old Arab tales are reworked to explain why there were abandoned cities in Arabia. The only new idea in the Koran is that Mohammed is prophet of Allah, all the world is to imitate him and that if you do not, you can be harmed. The horizon of the Koran goes no farther than Mohammed's world. It claims to be a universal text, but it is very provincial.

LOGIC

The Koran advances a logical system. Truth is determined by revelation. No fact or argument may refute the Koran. Logical persuasion is based upon repetition and continued assertion. Another part of the persuasion is personal attacks against those who resist Islam. The Koran advances its argument through threats against specific people and groups. If persuasion fails, then force may be used to settle the logical or political argument.

Another aspect of Koranic logic is the use of name calling and personal insults to advance the truth. The Koran, with its poetical language and repeated threats and physical violence, bases its logic on emotions.

Although its intellectual truth can be contradictory, the contradictions do not need to be resolved. Understanding apparent contradictions is a key to understanding Islamic logic. In the Koran, a contradiction does not prove an argument to be false. What appears to be logical contradictions are statements of duality that offer two true choices, depending upon the circumstances. This is a dualistic logic.

DUALITY

The constant theme of the Koran is the division between those who believe Mohammed, and those who don't. This sacred division is dualism; Kafirs are not fully human and fall under a separate moral code. The dualistic separation is in politics, culture and religion. This duality is carried further by two different approaches to the Kafir in the Koran of Mecca and the Koran of Medina.

Some verses of the Koran contradict each other, but the text states a principle for resolving the contradictions. The later verse abrogates (nullifies) the earlier verse. However, since the entire Koran comes from Allah, then all verses are true, and no verse is actually false. The later, contradictory verse is merely stronger than the earlier, weaker verse. In practice, both sides of a contradiction can be true—logical duality.

ETHICS

There is no unitary ethic such as the Golden Rule in the Koran. Since the ethical system of the Koran is dualistic, there cannot be a Golden Rule. How a person is treated depends upon his being a believer or an Kafir. There is one set of ethics for the believer and another set of ethics for the Kafir. Deceit, violence and force are acceptable against the Kafirs who resist the logic of the Koran. Believers are to be treated as brothers and sisters. Good is what advances Islam. Evil is whatever resists Islam.

POLITICS

The story of the Koran culminates in the dominance of political Islam. The Koran teaches that Islam is the perfect political system and is destined to rule the entire world. The governments and constitutions of the world must all submit to political Islam. If the political systems of the Kafirs do not submit, then force, jihad, may be used. All jihad is defensive, since refusing to submit to Islam is an offense against Allah. All Muslims must support the political action of jihad. This may take several forms—fighting, proselytizing or contributing money.

The basis of the Islamic dualistic legal code, the Sharia, is found in the Koran.

STATISTICS AND THE KORAN

One way to measure the importance of a topic is to notice how many resources are devoted to it. The simple act of counting how many words are devoted to a subject helps measure the importance of the subject.

FIGURE 17.1: THE AMOUNT OF TEXT DEVOTED TO KAFIR

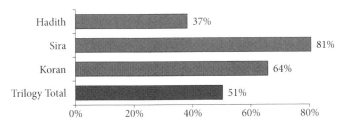

The Koran devotes 64% of the text to the Kafir[1]. The part of Islam that deals with the "outsider", the Kafir, is defined as political Islam. Since so much of the Koran is about the Kafir, the statistical conclusion is that Islam is primarily a political system, not a religious system.

The violence of the Meccan Koran is insults and torture in Hell after death. In Medina the Koran turns to the sword[2].

FIGURE 17.2: AMOUNT OF TRILOGY TEXT DEVOTED TO JIHAD

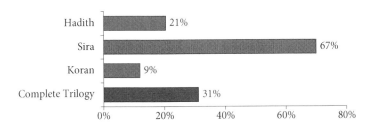

Mohammed preached the religion of Islam for 13 years in Mecca and garnered 150 followers. He was forced to move to Medina and became a politician and warrior. During the last 9 years of his life, he was involved in an event of violence every 6 weeks. When he died every Arab in his sphere

---

1   http://cspipublishing.com/statistical/TrilogyStats/AmtTxtDevoted-Kafir.html

2   http://cspipublishing.com/statistical/TrilogyStats/Percentage_of_Trilogy_Text_Devoted_to_Jihad.html

was a Muslim. Mohammed succeeded through politics, not religion. Using data from the Sira and history it is possible to draw a graph of the growth of Islam.

FIGURE 17.3 THE GROWTH OF ISLAM

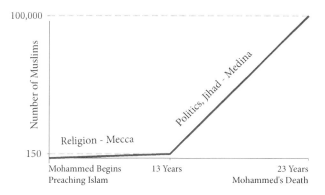

There are two distinct growth processes—religious and political. Teaching and religion grew at a rate of about 12 new Muslims per year. Politics and jihad grew at a rate of 10,000 new Muslims per year, an enormous increase. If Mohammed had continued with preaching the religion we can extrapolate that there would have been fewer than 300 Muslims when he died.

The dualistic Koran of Mecca has few negative verses about the Jews, but in Medina the Koran is vicious about the Jews[3]. The Koran of Medina has more Jew hatred than Hitler's *Mein Kampf*.

FIGURE 17.4: ANTI-JEWISH TEXT IN TRILOGY

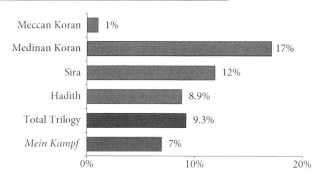

---

3   http://cspipublishing.com/statistical/TrilogyStats/Amt_anti-Jew_Text. html

The Koran's treatment of women is of interest[1]. This chart was prepared by collecting all of the verses that include any mention of women. These are then sorted into neutral, low status, high status and equal status. The neutral verses are not included in this study. The high status is given to mothers. The equal status occurs on Judgment day when men and women will be judged on the basis of their deeds. However, a woman will be judged on how well she obeyed her husband and was grateful to him.

FIGURE 17.5: STATUS OF WOMEN IN THE KORAN

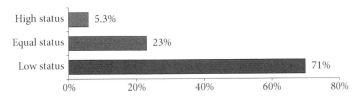

FOR MORE INFORMATION

Visit: www.politicalislam.com
www.cspii.com
Facebook: @BillWarnerAuthor
Twitter: @politicalislam.com
You Tube: Political Islam

---

1   http://cspipublishing.com/statistical/TrilogyStats/Womans_Status_in_the_Koran.html

Made in the USA
Columbia, SC
12 June 2017